I0050556

A STUDY ON NEPAL'S NATIONAL HEALTH INSURANCE PROGRAM

Rakesh Ayer, Suresh Tiwari, Shambhu Prasad Jnawali, and Rudi Van Dael

MAY 2024

ADB

ASIAN DEVELOPMENT BANK

© 2024 Asian Development Bank
6 ADB Avenue, Mandaluyong City, 1550 Metro Manila, Philippines
Tel +63 2 8632 4444; Fax +63 2 8636 2444
www.adb.org

Some rights reserved. Published in 2024.

ISBN 978-92-9270-700-2 (print); 978-92-9270-701-9 (PDF); 978-92-9270-702-6 (ebook)
Publication Stock No. TCS240257-2
DOI: http://dx.doi.org/10.22617/TCS240257-2

Notes:
In this publication, "$" refers to United States dollars.
ADB recognizes "Korea" as the Republic of Korea.

Cover design by Joe Mark Ganaban (photos by ADB and Rakesh Ayer).

CONTENTS

TABLES, FIGURES, AND BOXES

FOREWORD

One of the lessons learned from the global coronavirus disease (COVID-19) pandemic is the pivotal importance of having robust social protection mechanisms in place. The unprecedented health crisis highlighted the vulnerability of individuals and communities, as many who fell ill faced not only the physical toll of the virus but also the financial repercussions. This situation was even more pronounced in low-and middle-income countries such as Nepal. One of the key features of social protection systems, like health insurance, is to prevent populations from slipping into poverty during times of crisis such as the COVID-19 pandemic.

The National Health Insurance Program (NHIP) is the priority initiative of the Government of Nepal to achieve universal health coverage (UHC) and prevent households from falling back into poverty while seeking health care. The program was established in 2017 under the Health Insurance Act and has been considered a principal vehicle of the government to achieve the ambitious goal of UHC.

This study aims to provide an overview and assessment of the NHIP, including key challenges, and suggests considerations for strengthening the program. The study aims to support ongoing discussions on how to strengthen NHIP design and implementation.

The authors delve into the historical evolution of health insurance in Nepal, the country's context, major health outcomes, disparities in health outcomes based on socioeconomic status and location, and barriers to accessing health care services. It also includes an assessment of health care financing in Nepal compared with its regional counterparts. The authors use this background to set the stage for a comprehensive overview of the various aspects of the health insurance program, including a review of studies related to health insurance. The authors conclude the study with recommendations for strengthening the NHIP.

The Asian Development Bank (ADB) is committed to alleviate poverty and address inequality in Asia and the Pacific, as specified in its Strategy 2030. This study is part of ADB's commitment to support Nepal and other developing member countries in their pursuit of UHC to ensure equitable access to quality health services with financial protection.

Preparation of the study was part of the technical assistance attached to the countercyclical budgetary support of $250 million to the government under the COVID-19 Active Response and Expenditure Support (CARES) Program, which was mobilized in favor of the government's efforts to mitigate the impact of the COVID-19 pandemic. We would like to express our sincere gratitude to the Health Insurance Board for providing this opportunity to review the NHIP.

Gi Soon Song
Director, Human and Social Development Sectors Group
Asian Development Bank

Arnaud Cauchois
Country Director, Nepal Resident Mission
Asian Development Bank

MESSAGE

Government of Nepal
Health Insurance Board

Letter No.: 080181
Ref. No.: 1123

Phone No.:01-4100223
Toll Free: 16600111224
Teku, Kathmandu

The National Health Insurance Program (NHIP) stands as a crucial pillar in Nepal's journey toward shielding individuals from unexpected health care expenses, thereby managing risks upfront within the framework of government-provided social health protection. Launched in 2017 as part of Nepal's social security initiative, the program is overseen by the Health Insurance Board (HIB). Nepal's goal with this initiative is to move closer to achieving Universal Health Coverage (UHC) by 2030, a vital aspect of its Sustainable Development Goals.

Nepal's Constitution guarantees free basic health services and acknowledges health care as a fundamental right. Article 51 (H) of the Constitution emphasizes ensuring citizens' access to health insurance, safeguarding quality health care provision. The Health Insurance Act of 2017 was introduced to alleviate financial risks for insured individuals through pre-paid health insurance and to improve the efficiency and accountability of health care providers, thereby ensuring widespread access to health care.

Within less than a decade of its inception, the NHIP has extended coverage to over seven million individuals, a significant stride within the country's total population of 30 million. Nevertheless, intensified efforts are needed to cover more individuals and households. For this to happen, we will need strong support from all stakeholders, spanning government and non-government agencies, as well as development partners. Among various prioritized actions, these organizations can support the HIB by facilitating capacity building, strengthening claims management processes, supporting evidence-based policy formulation, integrating updated digital technologies, and fostering research.

I extend my appreciation to the Asian Development Bank team for their contributions toward the realization of this study. The study adeptly synthesizes the evolution of health insurance in Nepal, and offers useful recommendations, which I believe will help strengthen the NHIP's foundations.

Finally, I would like to extend my sincere thanks to all stakeholders whose support was instrumental in materializing this study. This includes, but is not limited to, insured members, enrollment assistants, enrollment officers, and provincial coordinators.

Dr. Damodar Basaula
Executive Director
Health Insurance Board

ACKNOWLEDGMENTS

The authors extend their sincere gratitude to all stakeholders in the National Health Insurance Program, with special appreciation for the officials at the Health Insurance Board whose support has been invaluable.

The authors would like to express their heartfelt thanks to the following individuals whose time and insightful comments greatly enhanced the quality of this study: Asian Development Bank (ADB) peer reviewer Dinesh Arora, principal health specialist; and Sonalini Khetrapal, senior health specialist and Dai-Ling Chen, health specialist, for their invaluable insights. Special recognition is due to Anne Thapa Magar and Prabina Thapa Magar, operations assistants, who supported with editing of the final draft.

The study has also benefited from the insights shared by the Deutsche Gesellschaft für Internationale Zusammenarbeit (GIZ) team and the Health Nutrition and Population team at the World Bank Nepal country office.

Finally, the authors would like to express their appreciation to the Ministry of Health and Population for their guidance and feedback. We are specially grateful to the Ministry of Finance for entrusting ADB to implement the COVID-19 Active Response and Expenditure Support (CARES) program and the associated technical assistance activities, of which this study is an integral part.

AUTHORS

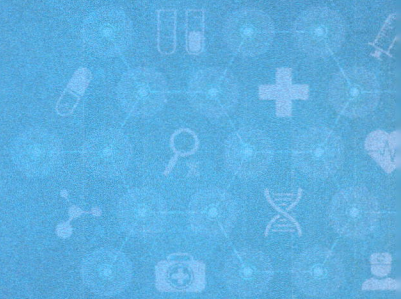

Rakesh Ayer, PhD, MSc, specializes in human capital development and financing, with a deep passion for assisting low-and middle-income countries in achieving universal health coverage (UHC) and advancing universal social protection. Ayer earned his doctor of philosophy (PhD) degree from the University of Tokyo and possesses over 13 years of experience in global health and human capital development. Ayer has worked with the Asian Development Bank (ADB), the World Bank, the World Health Organization, and the Joint United Nations Program on HIV/AIDS (UNAIDS). Ayer has also held key positions in government agencies, extensively collaborating with several line ministries and public agencies. Most recently, the Ministry of Health and Population in Nepal nominated him as one of the key experts to spearhead the development of the Health Insurance Road Map 2030. Ayer has authored over 20 scholarly articles in esteemed international journals, garnering numerous citations. His research contributions span diverse areas, including human capital development and financing, UHC, health financing, development assistance to health, impact evaluation, enhancement of health service quality, infectious diseases response, and the formulation of health and social protection policies aligned with the Sustainable Development Goals. Ayer has diverse work experiences in countries including Nepal, Thailand, the Philippines, Switzerland, and Japan. Currently, he serves as a health and financing expert consultant at ADB. Simultaneously, Ayer holds the role of a visiting global health scientist at the University of Tokyo.

Suresh Tiwari, PhD, is a seasoned professional in the fields of public policy, public health, and governance. He has worked in several countries, including Nepal, Thailand, Bangladesh, Cambodia, Australia, and Canada, gaining expertise in formulating public policy, national strategic plans, and emergency policies for events such as earthquakes and the coronavirus disease (COVID-19) pandemic. He has also been involved in developing financing and response plans, particularly in relation to the COVID-19 pandemic. With a career spanning over 20 years, Tiwari has been actively engaged in policy evaluation, designing social protection schemes, developing health financing strategies, and implementing health insurance policies. Additionally, he has worked on developing internal control systems, curriculum development, and capacity building for government institutions and civil society organizations. Tiwari has conducted numerous studies related to demand- and supply-side financing, epidemiology, and the general characteristics of health systems. He has a particular focus on pro-poor health financing, aiming to ensure equitable access to health care for all segments of society. Currently, Tiwari serves as the country director of Oxford Policy Management Nepal, where he continues to contribute his expertise in public policy, public health, governance.

Shambhu Prasad Jnawali, MPH, MA, is a former Ministry of Health and Population official in Nepal. Over the course of over a 30-year career, he has contributed through diverse managerial and implementation roles in the health sector of Nepal. He was a senior public health administrator at the Health Insurance Board, where he oversaw various aspects of health insurance program strengthening, ranging from fiscal planning to formulation of program-related guidelines, standards, and policies. His responsibilities also encompassed organizing national-level meetings, workshops, and training sessions.

Rudi Van Dael, PhD, is a principal social sector specialist outposted at the ADB Nepal Resident Mission. He focuses on ADB support provided to the social sector in Nepal, mainly education and health. Van Dael also was the ADB focal for the COVID-19 support in Nepal. Previously, he was the principal portfolio management specialist based in the ADB Nepal Resident Mission. From 2010 until 2019, Van Dael was a social sector specialist in ADB working on various education projects in Bangladesh, Indonesia, and Nepal. Van Dael was involved in studies on using human-centered design, entrepreneurship programs, skills for the electricity sector, minimum service standards in education, and subsidized employment programs. Van Dael has a diploma in computing science, a master's degree in public administration, and a PhD in sociology.

ABBREVIATIONS

ADB	–	Asian Development Bank
BHS	–	basic health services
CARES	–	COVID-19 Active Response and Expenditure Support
CHE	–	current health expenditure
COVID-19	–	coronavirus disease
FY	–	fiscal year
GDP	–	gross domestic product
GHED	–	Global Health Expenditure Database
HIB	–	Health Insurance Board
IMR	–	infant mortality rate
MOF	–	Ministry of Finance
MOHP	–	Ministry of Health and Population
NDHS	–	Nepal Demographic and Health Survey
NHIP	–	National Health Insurance Program
NMR	–	neonatal mortality rate
NRs	–	Nepalese rupees
NSO	–	National Statistics Office
OOPS	–	out-of-pocket health expenditures
PHCC	–	primary health care center
SDG	–	Sustainable Development Goal
UHC	–	universal health coverage
WDI	–	World Development Indicators
WHO	–	World Health Organization

CURRENCY EQUIVALENT

$1.00 = NRs132.60

NRs1.00 = $0.0075

EXECUTIVE SUMMARY

Nepal has made significant strides in health care, with improvements in life expectancy and reductions in under-5 mortality rates and maternal mortality ratios. To further improve access to health care, health outcomes, and the quality of health care services equitably among its population while shielding them from falling into poverty during health care utilization, the Government of Nepal has long embarked on developing health insurance in the country. The development of health insurance in Nepal has been gradual, with initiatives dating back to 1976. The Social Health Insurance Policy, launched in 2016 and integrated into the Health Insurance Board (HIB) in 2017, aimed to provide quality health care services and protect households from financial hardships.

The National Health Insurance Program (NHIP) under the HIB, implemented nationwide, provides financial risk protection through health insurance to the Nepalese population. The design of the health insurance scheme follows a typical approach used by low- and middle-income countries transitioning away from user fees. The NHIP receives financial contributions from both the government and its insured members in the form of insurance premiums, which must be renewed annually. The current annual premium is NRs3,500 ($26.40) per family, with an additional NRs700 ($5.30) fee for each additional insured member beyond five family members. The government provides subsidies on the premiums for certain targeted groups: ultra-poor, senior citizens, severely disabled, leprosy patients, multidrug-resistant tuberculosis patients, and HIV/AIDS patient households receive a full subsidy. The Government of Nepal provides 50% subsidy on premiums of female community health volunteers. Members of NHIP are entitled to free care at empaneled health facilities up to a maximum of NRs100,000 ($754) per family annually. Families with more than five members receive an additional benefit of NRs20,000 ($150.80) for each additional member, not exceeding a maximum benefit ceiling of NRs200,000 ($1,508.30) per family.

However, challenges persist, including low population coverage (23%), limited risk pooling, stagnant financing, lack of financial sustainability assessment, inadequate local-level empanelment of health facilities, limited digitalization of the NHIP functions, weak HIB capacity, and insufficient government ownership toward strengthening NHIP. Concerns also exist regarding moral hazards, unmeasured impacts on out-of-pocket health spending, and an outdated benefit package.

Some key recommendations for strengthening NHIP include updating the benefit package, expanding population coverage to incorporate all ultra-poor citizens and underserved provinces, focusing on expanding enrollment rates, implementation of demand-generating activities, and improving risk pooling. There is a need to empanel more health facilities in NHIP, as most local levels currently do not have NHIP-listed health facilities. An assessment to conduct the feasibility of health facilities for their potential empanelment could support this objective.

NHIP's functions and implementation process can be made efficient and effective with the incorporation of updated information technology tools. This can be also achieved by making the information system of NHIP interoperable with the information systems of other social protection schemes, thereby reducing costs and streamlining health financing mechanisms.

Finally, strengthening NHIP is essential for Nepal's goal of achieving universal health care. Addressing the identified challenges and implementing proposed recommendations can enhance the NHIP's effectiveness, ensuring equitable access to quality health care for all citizens.

INTRODUCTION

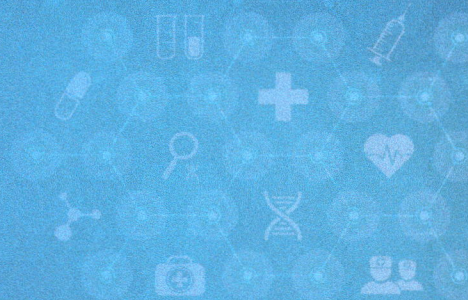

The development of health insurance in Nepal has been a gradual process with several initiatives implemented over time. In 1976, the first health insurance scheme was introduced in Patan Hospital in Lalitpur District. In 2000, a similar initiative was implemented by BP Koirala Institute of Health Sciences in 17 different communities of Morang and Sunsari districts. In 2003, the Government of Nepal implemented a health insurance program in six primary health care centers (PHCCs). In 2007, the government introduced a free health care program which provided all health care services up to PHCC level as well as 35 basic medicines for free. Despite this initiative, the financial burden of health care expenditure on families continued to increase, which led to the introduction of a Social Health Insurance Policy in 2013. In 2015, the Social Health Security Development Committee was formed, and the Social Health Insurance Program was launched in 2016. The program was later integrated into the Health Insurance Board (HIB) in 2017, with the goal of providing quality health care services, protecting households from financial hardship, and increasing accountability among health care providers. The program was expanded to 65 districts and 636 local levels in 2021. It was implemented in all 77 districts by the end of 2022 (HIB 2022).

The major objectives of this study are as follows: (i) to provide the country context, major health outcomes, and health financing status in Nepal; (ii) to outline different aspects of the National Health Insurance Program (NHIP) including its overview, governance and budgeting, coverage, benefit package, and policy environment; and (iii) to provide some recommendations for strengthening of the NHIP.[1]

---

[1] The National Relief Program (NRP) was launched by the Government of Nepal to address the consequences of the coronavirus disease (COVID-19). The NRP, approved on 29 March 2020, aimed to provide (i) support for health response measures, (ii) delivery of social protection and relief programs, and (iii) economic support for impacted sectors. The Asian Development Bank (ADB) supported the implementation of the NRP through the COVID-19 Active Response and Expenditure Support program. ADB provided technical assistance to the government for the management, monitoring, and reporting of NRP. The assistance included providing policy advice on medium-term interventions to enhance the health system. To this end, the government asked ADB to conduct studies to identify gaps in the NHIP for improved service delivery. This study aims to achieve these goals. This study was in part prepared by the Oxford Policy Management and commissioned by ADB.

Figure 1: Historical Evolution of Health Insurance in Nepal

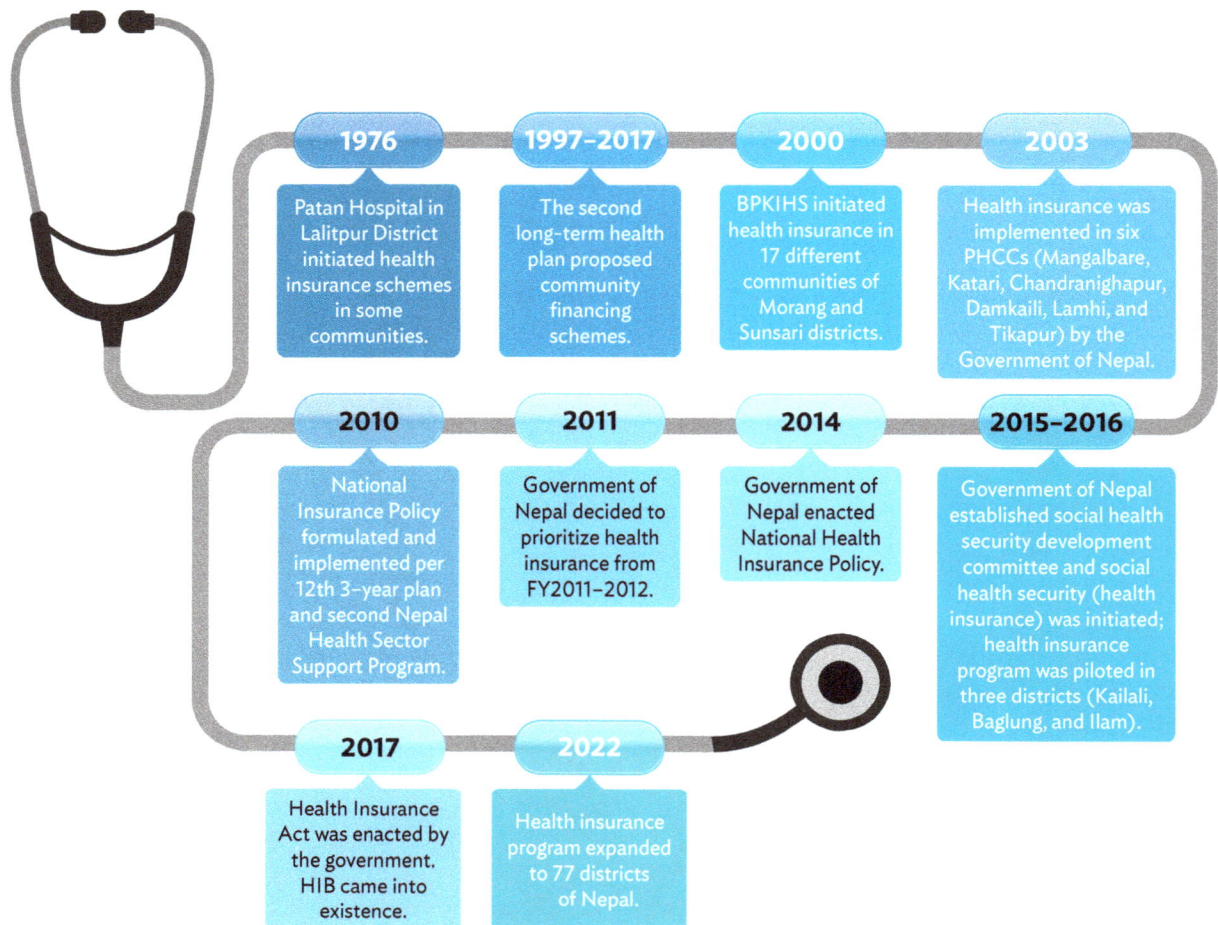

1976
Patan Hospital in Lalitpur District initiated health insurance schemes in some communities.

1997–2017
The second long-term health plan proposed community financing schemes.

2000
BPKIHS initiated health insurance in 17 different communities of Morang and Sunsari districts.

2003
Health insurance was implemented in six PHCCs (Mangalbare, Katari, Chandranighapur, Damkaili, Lamhi, and Tikapur) by the Government of Nepal.

2010
National Insurance Policy formulated and implemented per 12th 3-year plan and second Nepal Health Sector Support Program.

2011
Government of Nepal decided to prioritize health insurance from FY2011–2012.

2014
Government of Nepal enacted National Health Insurance Policy.

2015–2016
Government of Nepal established social health security development committee and social health security (health insurance) was initiated; health insurance program was piloted in three districts (Kailali, Baglung, and Ilam).

2017
Health Insurance Act was enacted by the government. HIB came into existence.

2022
Health insurance program expanded to 77 districts of Nepal.

BPKIHS = BP Koirala Institute of Health Sciences, FY = fiscal year, HIB = Health Insurance Board, PHCC = primary health care center.
Source: HIB 2022. HIB Annual Report 2020.

Country Context

Nepal is a landlocked federal democratic republic in South Asia with an estimated population of 29.2 million (National Statistics Office [NSO], 2021 census) and a total land area of 147,516 square kilometers. Its population is diverse, comprising various ethnic groups spanning from the plains in the south to the high mountains in the north. Although 34% of the population lives in rural areas (NSO, 2021 census), Nepal is undergoing rapid urbanization, and prior to the coronavirus disease (COVID-19), had one of the world's fastest-growing economies.

Nepal is classified as a lower-middle-income country according to the World Bank's income level categorization of countries. Nepal's gross national income per capita reached $1,340 in 2022, higher than that of Ethiopia ($1,020) and Tajikistan ($1,210) (World Development Indicators [WDI] 2024).

The country exhibited robust economic growth, achieving gross domestic product (GDP) of 9% in 2017, 7.6% in 2018, and 6.7% in 2019 (WDI 2023). This marked a substantial improvement from the average annual growth rates of 2% between 2000 and 2007 and 3.3% between 2008 and 2017. In cumulative per capita terms, Nepal's economy expanded by 61% between 2000 and 2017. However, the COVID-19 pandemic had a detrimental impact, causing a 2.4% contraction in GDP (ADB 2023). The economy has since been on the path to recovery, with GDP growing by 4.8% in 2021 and 5.6% in 2022 (ADB 2023). The service sector dominates Nepal's economy, constituting 62% of GDP in 2022, while agriculture comprised 24% of GDP and industry 14% (Ministry of Finance 2022). Despite an overall increase in the public debt, the country's risk of debt distress was rated *low* in terms of debt sustainability by a joint review from the World Bank and International Monetary Fund in 2020 (World Bank-IMF 2020).

The Government of Nepal is committed to achieving the Sustainable Development Goals (SDGs) by 2030, particularly in improving the health delivery system, which is now under the purview of subnational governments. However, this commitment comes at a time when unstable economic performance, recovering from the aftermath of COVID-19, and the ongoing transition to a federal system may threaten the government's ability to finance and expand health care services.

Major Health Outcomes

Nepal has made significant strides in improving its health outcomes over the past few decades. Life expectancy steadily increased from 38 years in 1960 (WDI 2023) to 70.5 years in 2022 (UNDP 2022), while the under-5 mortality rate dropped from 325 per 1,000 live births in 1960 to 33 per 1,000 live births in 2022 (Nepal Demographic and Health Survey, 2022) (Figure 2). Additionally, the percentage of births attended by skilled provider rose from 10% in 1996 to 80% in 2022 (NDHS 2022), and the maternal mortality ratio significantly decreased from 553 to 151 per 100,000 live births between 2000 and 2021 (WDI, 2023) (NSO 2021). These trends suggest that Nepal is making progress toward achieving the SDGs for child and maternal health by 2030.

Figure 2: Improvements in Major Health Outcomes over the Past Decades in Nepal

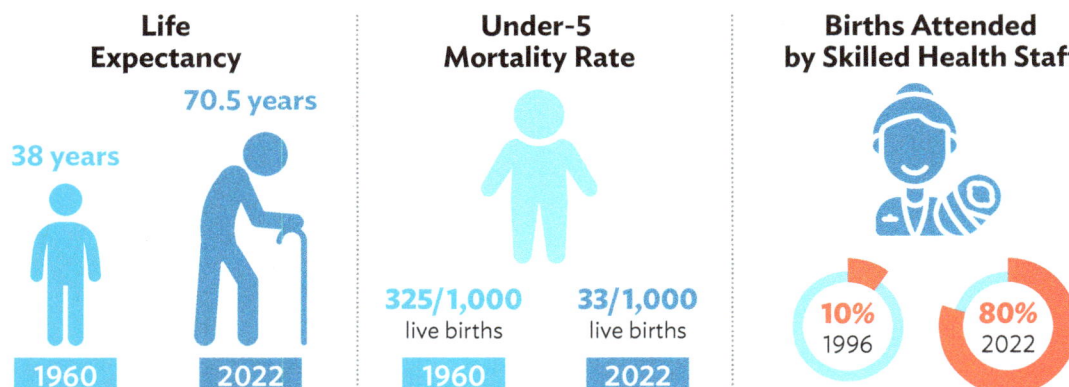

Life Expectancy

38 years — 1960
70.5 years — 2022

Under-5 Mortality Rate

325/1,000 live births — 1960
33/1,000 live births — 2022

Births Attended by Skilled Health Staff

10% — 1996
80% — 2022

Source: UNDP 2022. WDI 2023. Nepal Demographic and Health Survey 2022.

Compared to its regional neighbors and countries with a similar income level, Nepal's health indicators perform relatively well. For instance, in 1960, Nepal had one of the highest under-5 mortality rates among its regional comparators, but by 2022, it had surpassed Pakistan in this regard and was below the South Asia average of 37 per 1,000 live births. Furthermore, Nepal's population health indicators such as life expectancy at birth, fertility rate, and maternal mortality ratio are better than expected for a country with its income level.

Table 1: Selected Health and Population Outcomes, by Country and Region

Country	Births Attended by Skilled Health Staff, 2015–2021 (%)	Life Expectancy (2020)	Fertility Rate (2020)	Under-5 Mortality Rate (per 1,000 live births, 2021)	Maternal Mortality Ratio (per 100,000 live births, 2017)
Afghanistan	62	62.6	4.2	55.7	638
Bangladesh	59	72.0	2.0	27.3	173
Bhutan	96	71.6	1.9	26.7	183
India	89	70.2	2.2	30.6	145
Maldives	100	79.9	1.8	6.0	53
Nepal	**80**[a]	**70.5**[b]	**1.8**	**33**[a]	**151**[b]
Pakistan	68	66.3	3.4	63.3	140
Sri Lanka	100	76.4	2.2	6.7	36
South Asia average	**82**	**69.7**	**2.3**	**37.1**	**163**
Low-income countries	**67**	**62.9**	**4.5**	**67.4**	**453**
Lower-middle-income countries	**78**	**68.6**	**2.7**	**43.7**	**253**

[a] Data from the Nepal Demographic and Health Survey conducted in 2022.
[b] Data from the UNDP SDGs progress report 2016–2019.
Source: World Development Indicators, World Bank 2023, * Data from the National Census conducted in 2021, National Statistics Office.

While there have been positive developments in health outcomes, there are still challenges that need to be addressed. Specifically, there are disparities in key health indicators between wealth quintiles and provinces. Box 1 describes the differences in infant mortality rate, neonatal mortality rate, and under-5 mortality rate across wealth quintiles and provinces. Children in the middle and lower wealth quintiles experience the highest rates of infant mortality, neonatal mortality, under-5 mortality, and stunting compared to those in the richer and upper quintiles. Health facility child delivery is also lowest among the population in the middle to poorest quintiles, compared to the fourth and richest quintile.

Box 1: Disparities in Health Outcomes across Wealth Quintiles and Provinces in Nepal

Disparities in health outcomes are a major challenge in Nepal. Table 2 (page 6) highlights these disparities across different wealth quintiles. According to the data, 98% of women in the richest wealth quintile delivered their babies at a health facility, compared to only 66% of women in the poorest quintile. Similarly, the prevalence of childhood stunting is higher in the poorest quintile, with 37% of children affected, compared to 13 % in the richest quintile.

Table 4 (page 7) displays the prevalence of stunting and mortality rates across different provinces. Karnali has the highest prevalence of stunting, with 36% children affected, followed by Madhesh 29% and Sudurpaschim at 28%. These rates are higher than the national average of 25% and those observed in other provinces. Additionally, neonatal mortality rates (NMR) in Sudurpaschim (37 deaths per 1,000 live births), Madhesh (27), and Karnali (26) are highest, as well as under-5 mortality rates (Sudurpaschim is at 49, Karnali at 46, and Madhesh at 43). Gandaki (19 deaths per 1,000 live births) and Bagmati (21) have the lowest infant mortality rates (IMR) and under-5 mortality rates (Gandaki at 23 and Bagmati at 24). Gandaki has the lowest NMR at 8 per 1,000 live births.

Table 4 also highlights disparities in health facility child delivery across different provinces. Bagmati and Gandaki have the highest rate of institutional delivery, with 88% of women in both provinces delivering their child at a health facility, followed by Sudurpaschim at 87%, Lumbini at 84%, Koshi at 82%, and Karnali at 72%. In Madhesh, only 67% of women give birth at a health facility, the lowest among all provinces in Nepal.

The Sustainable Development Goals aim for all countries to reduce their NMR to below 12 per 1,000 live births and their under-5 mortality rate below 25 per 1,000 live births by 2030. With overall NMR at 21 and under-5 mortality rate at 33, Nepal needs to build on its past gains while addressing significant disparities between wealth quintiles and provinces. For example, as shown in Table 2, the NMR is 31 among children in the second wealth quintile, compared to 13 among children in the richest quintile. Similarly, the under-5 mortality rate is 53 among children in the lowest wealth index quintile and 16 among children in the richest quintile.

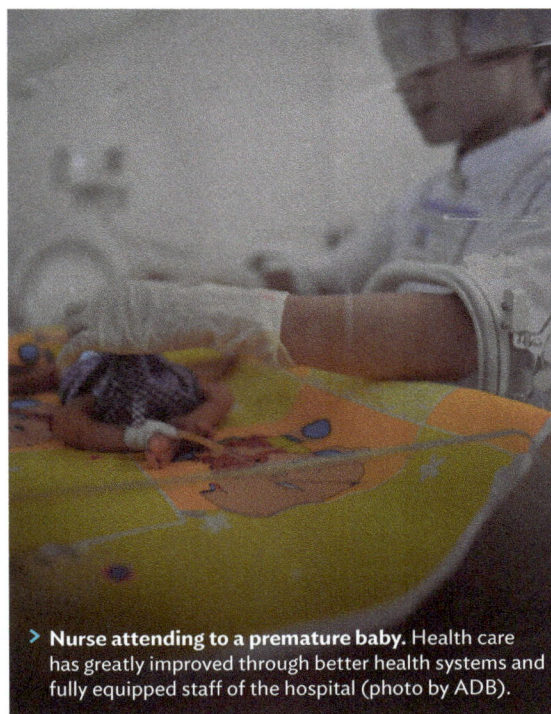

> **Nurse attending to a premature baby.** Health care has greatly improved through better health systems and fully equipped staff of the hospital (photo by ADB).

Source: Nepal Demographic and Health Survey 2022.

Table 2: Selected Health Outcomes by Wealth Quintiles

Wealth Quintile	NMR	IMR	Under-5 MR	Health Facility Child Delivery (%)	Childhood Stunting (%)
Lowest	26	45	53	65.8	37
Second	31	41	50	73.2	28
Middle	21	26	30	79.6	22
Fourth	17	23	28	87.1	18
Highest	13	15	16	97.6	13
Overall	**21**	**28**	**33**	**79.4**	**25**

MR=mortality rate, IMR = infant mortality rate, NMR = neonatal mortality rate.
Note: NMR, IMR, and Under-5 MR per 1,000 live births.
Source: Nepal Demographic and Health Survey 2022.

As shown in Box 1, health status in relation to key health care indicators along with the utilization of health care services and institutional delivery remains low among the population from the poorest wealth index quintiles and in Madhesh and Karnali provinces. Therefore, distribution of population according to wealth index quintile by province shown in Table 3 provides an important understanding regarding the link between provincial disparities and wealth index quintiles in key health care indicators.

As shown in Table 3, much of the population in Karnali (65.9%) and Sudurpaschim (40.6%) fall under the poorest wealth index quintile category. On the other hand, nearly half of the population in Bagmati (43.4%) is in the richest wealth index quintile category. While the prevalence of stunting is 36% in Karnali, it is 18% in Bagmati. In addition, institutional delivery in Karnali is only 72%, whereas it is 88.3% in Bagmati. Moreover, under-5 mortality is 46 in Karnali whereas it is 24 in Bagmati (Table 4). This suggests that socioeconomic disparities remain as the major barrier to achieving key health care indicator goals set out in SDGs and attaining universal health coverage (UHC) in Nepal.

Table 3: Distribution of Population in Different Provinces in Nepal by Wealth Quintiles
(%)

Province	Lowest	Second	Middle	Fourth	Highest
Koshi	22.6	23.7	19.6	21.4	12.7
Madhesh	9.6	28.2	29.0	21.7	11.6
Bagmati	11.6	11.8	13.6	19.6	43.4
Gandaki	16.6	16.4	19.6	23.3	24.2
Lumbini	15.5	20.4	23.7	22.2	18.2
Karnali	65.9	13.3	7.2	8.2	5.5
Sudurpaschim	40.6	19.8	16.1	14.4	9.2

Source: Nepal Demographic and Health Survey 2022.

Table 4: Selected Health Outcomes by Province

Province	NMR	IMR	Under-5 MR	Health Facility Delivery (%)	Childhood Stunting (%)
Koshi	20	28	34	81.5	20
Madhesh	27	38	43	66.8	29
Bagmati	18	21	24	88.3	18
Gandaki	8	19	23	87.8	20
Lumbini	24	34	41	84.4	25
Karnali	26	36	46	72.4	36
Sudurpaschim	37	40	49	86.8	28
Overall	**21**	**28**	**33**	**79.4**	**25**

MR=mortality rate, IMR = infant mortality rate, NMR = neonatal mortality rate.
Note: NMR, IMR, and Under-5 MR per 1,000 live births.
Source: Nepal Demographic and Health Survey 2022.

The Asia Foundation conducted the Survey of Nepali People in four different years (2017, 2018, 2020, and 2022) using the same approach, i.e., a nationally representative sample of about 7,000 respondents was chosen, and they were asked about their opinions on various topics of public concern, including public outlook, security, identity, governance, politics, economics, and access to information. While the sampling approach used in the earlier surveys was retained, the selection of wards, households, and respondents was randomized and varied in each round of the survey. The Survey of Nepali People assessed the perceptions of respondents on the roles of mother tongue, ethnicity, and gender to accessing health care in Nepal. The survey results in Table 5 show significant decline in these barriers since the implementation of federalism in 2017. Within the mandate of federalism is the concept of health decentralization, which involves bringing health care services closer to the people they serve. This allows subnational governments to establish strong governance and accountability mechanisms and to concentrate their efforts on screening, primary care, referral systems, and local needs. Although it is too soon to determine how decentralization has affected health equity, the experiences of local communities thus far can provide insight into the benefits and challenges associated with the transition toward a more federalist approach to health care in Nepal.

In 2017, over half of Nepal's population faced difficulties accessing local health services because their native language was not Nepali, which was a primary language for such services in Nepal. Of these individuals, 25.8% perceived this as a disadvantage when accessing health services in 2017; this figure decreased to 15.4% in 2018 and 11.7% in 2022. Similarly, the proportion of Nepalese who believe that their ethnicity is a disadvantage when obtaining health services decreased from 5.3% in 2017 to 1.8% in 2022. Gender was also found to be a disadvantage in accessing health services for 5.1% of women in 2017 compared to 2.4% in 2022. Federalism may have been a positive force in improving health care access by reducing these social barriers. This decline in social barriers while accessing health services was also observed across the provinces. For example, in 2022, nearly 20% of respondents in Madhesh and 15% in Lumbini considered mother tongue to be a significant disadvantage when accessing health services. This is a significant improvement compared to 2017, when nearly 38% of Madhesh respondents and 27% in Lumbini were asked the same question. Similar progress has been noted in reducing barriers due to ethnicity and gender. This suggests that the opportunities from federalism seem to have been effective in reducing social barriers while accessing health services in Nepal.

Table 5: Perceived Problems in Assessing Health Services Associated with Social Disadvantages
(%)

		Koshi	Madhesh	Bagmati	Gandaki	Lumbini	Karnali	Sudurpaschim	Nepal (overall)
Mother tongue	2017	18.9	37.6	14.9	7.6	27.0	2.4	16.5	**25.8**
	2018	4.5	21.3	6.8	8.9	25.3	0.0	11.6	**15.4**
	2020	4.5	22.6	11.1	9.2	24.5	0.0	7.5	**15.7**
	2022	4.5	19.0	3.2	0.8	14.5	0.0	8.3	**11.7**
Ethnicity	2017	5.1	6.2	2.5	3.4	9.0	3.6	3.6	**5.3**
	2018	1.7	6.8	0.9	1.7	4.3	3.6	2.2	**3.1**
	2020	1.5	7.2	2.3	1.1	5.4	1.7	2.4	**3.6**
	2022	0.8	3.8	0.0	0.9	3.2	1.8	1.5	**1.8**
Gender	2017	4.1	6.5	2.3	3.8	7.8	7.9	4.8	**5.1**
	2018	2.2	11.9	1.3	1.3	5.0	7.6	1.1	**4.5**
	2020	1.6	17.6	1.3	0.3	5.8	3.8	2.5	**5.7**
	2022	1.1	6.7	0.8	0.4	2.3	2.0	1.4	**2.4**

Source: Asia Foundation, A Survey of Nepali People (2017, 2018, 2020, 2022).

Disparities in accessing health care services and health outcomes are closely intertwined with health financing mechanisms. As discussed above, people in lower income brackets and inhabiting remote and underserved provinces such as Karnali, Sudurpaschim, Lumbini, and Madhesh often have poorer outcomes compared to those with higher incomes and residing in provinces such as Bagmati, Koshi, and Gandaki. This is partly due to the fact that these population groups have less access to health care services, including preventative and curative care services which can result in delayed access to health care and poorer health outcomes. Health financing challenges such as low public spending on health, limited health insurance coverage, and higher out-of-pocket health expenditures (OOPS) can also exacerbate these disparities. For example, individuals in these provinces without insurance coverage or with high deductibles may delay seeking health care, leading to more severe health problems and increased health care costs in the long run. Other indirect and opportunity costs associated with health-care-seeking behavior in these regions (e.g., transportation cost, long travel time to health facilities, and accommodation expenses) also hinder timely health care delivery. Addressing disparities in health outcomes and health financing mechanisms are crucial to improving overall population health and ensuring that everyone has access to quality health care.

Status of Health Care Financing

As shown in Table 6, Nepal's current health expenditure (CHE) of $65, compared to the South Asia average of $205.8, is significantly lower. Nepal's OOPS as a percentage of CHE (51.3%) is also higher compared to the South Asia average (48.2%). As noted earlier, higher OOPS can make households vulnerable to catastrophic health expenditures and can lead them to impoverishment. Higher OOPS is often associated with lower levels of public spending on health. Nepal's public spending on health as a percentage of CHE is only 33.2%, which is slightly lower than the South Asia average of 36.5%. Nepal's OOPS is lower than that of Afghanistan (77.2%), Bangladesh (73%), and Pakistan (57.5%).

Table 6: Comparison of Key Health Financing Indicators among South Asian Association for Regional Cooperation Countries in 2021

Country	CHE per Capita ($)	Public Spending on Health as % of CHE	OOPS as % of CHE	GDP per Capita (Current)
Afghanistan	81	3.3	77.2	373
Bangladesh	58	16.9	73.0	2,450
Bhutan	120	57.4	18.8	3,132
India	74	34.3	49.8	2,256
Maldives	1,039	71.6	14.3	10,354
Nepal	**65**	**33.2**	**51.3**	**1,340**
Pakistan	43	29.0	57.5	1,480
Sri Lanka	166	46.4	43.6	4,087
South Asia average	**205.8**	**36.5**	**48.2**	**3,167**

CHE = current health expenditure, GDP = gross domestic product, OOPS = out-of-pocket health expenditures.
Source: WHO GHED 2023.

In 2021, as shown in Figure 3, Nepal's OOPS of over 50% is high and can be a precursor for inefficient and ineffective health system functioning. Despite all efforts, Nepal's social health insurance schemes contribute only 3% to the CHE. This is followed by government transfers at 33.1% and external aid at 13%. Other sources make up the remaining 4.64% (Table 7) (World Health Organization Global Health Expenditure Database [WHO GHED] 2023). Development partners provide both on- and off-budget support to the Government of Nepal. For example, most financial support from ADB and the World Bank is on budget. Bilateral partners, including Deutsche Gesellschaft für Internationale Zusammenarbeit (GIZ) German Agency for International Cooperation and United States Agency for International Development, also provide on-budget support to the government.

Figure 3: Contribution of Different Sources in Health Expenditures in Nepal (%)

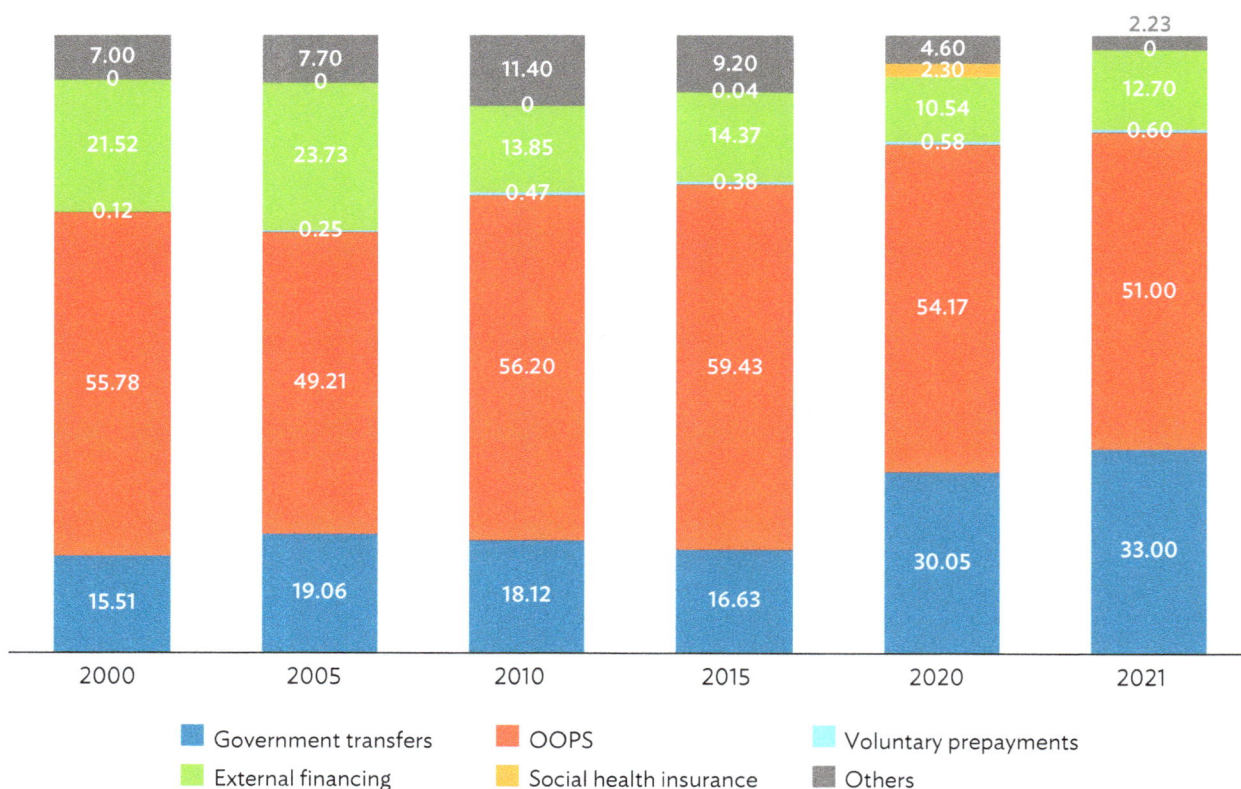

Source	2000	2005	2010	2015	2020	2021
Others	7.00	7.70	11.40	9.20	4.60	2.23
Social health insurance	0	0	0	0.04	2.30	0
External financing	21.52	23.73	13.85	14.37	10.54	12.70
Voluntary prepayments	0.12	0.25	0.47	0.38	0.58	0.60
OOPS	55.78	49.21	56.20	59.43	54.17	51.00
Government transfers	15.51	19.06	18.12	16.63	30.05	33.00

Legend: Government transfers, OOPS, Voluntary prepayments, External financing, Social health insurance, Others

OOPS = out-of-pocket health expenditures.
Note: For zeros in the above figure, no contribution from these sources in the given years.
Source: WHO GHED 2023.

Table 7: Trend in Key Health Financing Indicators of Nepal

Indicators	2000	2005	2010	2015	2020	2021
Public health expenditure (in % of GDP)*					1.0	1.1
CHE as % GDP	3	4	4	5	5	5
CHE per Capita ($)	8	14	30	47	58	65
Public health expenditure as % CHE	16	19	18	17	30	33
OOPS as % of CHE	56	49	56	59	54	51
External health expenditure as % of CHE	22	24	14	14	11	13
Social health insurance as % of CHE	0	0	0	0	2	3

CHE = current health expenditure, GDP = gross domestic product, OOPS = out-of-pocket health expenditures.
Source: WHO GHED 2023. *IMF.

In Nepal, fiscal year (FY) begins in mid-July. In FY2017/2018, three-quarters of the total OOPS by households, equivalent to 75.7% of NRs84,820 million were, spent on purchasing medicines and medical products from retailers such as pharmacies and dispensaries. Private hospitals received 9.2% of the OOPS, while public hospitals received only 6.2% of total household OOPS in the same period (Ministry of Health and Population [MOHP] 2020).

The majority of household OOPS in FY2017/2018 were dedicated to health care services related to noncommunicable diseases, which accounted for 54.6% of OOPS. Other and unspecified diseases and health conditions came next at 18.3%, followed by infectious and parasitic disease at 13.6%, injuries at 10.7%, reproductive health at 2.6%, and nutritional deficiencies at 0.3% (MOHP 2022) (Figure 4). However, there is currently a gap in evidence regarding further analysis of those unspecified health conditions. Also, data are lacking on indirect and opportunity costs associated with health-care-seeking behavior such as transportation expenses, long travel time to health facilities, and accommodation expenses.

Figure 4: Household Out-of-Pocket Health Spending by Diseases or Health Conditions (%)

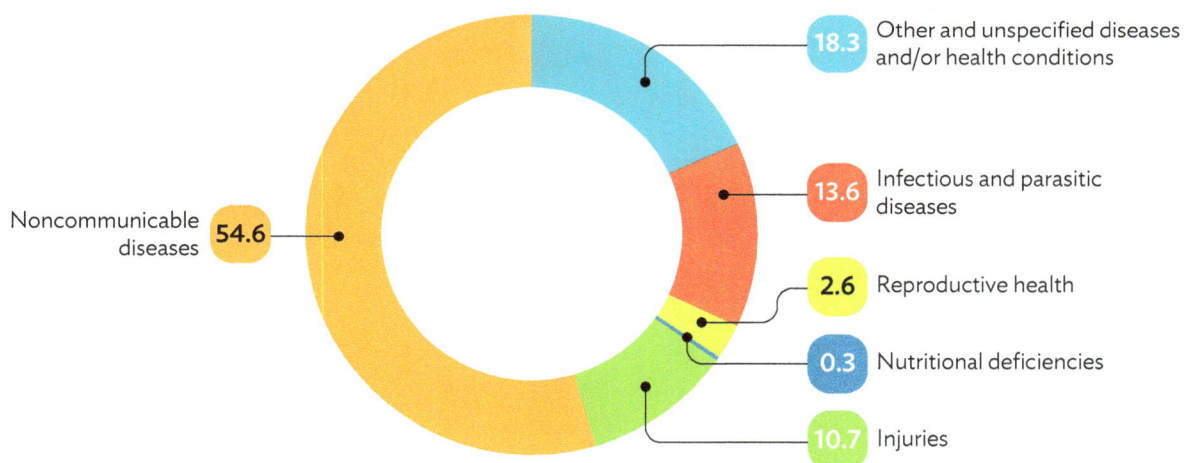

Source: National Health Accounts 2017–2018, Ministry of Health and Population.

Health care provision factors refer to the assessed inputs utilized in the production and distribution of health care services. Within the realm of health care expenditure classification, a significant portion (40.4% of CHE) is allocated toward pharmaceuticals and medical supplies. Health care services expenditure accounts for 33.7% of the CHE, excluding laboratory and imaging services, which make up 4.2% of the CHE. Compensation for health workers, encompassing wages, salaries, and other related expenses, represents approximately 11.8% of CHE, with the majority originating from the public sector (Figure 5).

Figure 5: Current Health Expenditure Distribution by Factors of Health Care Provision in 2017–2018
(%)

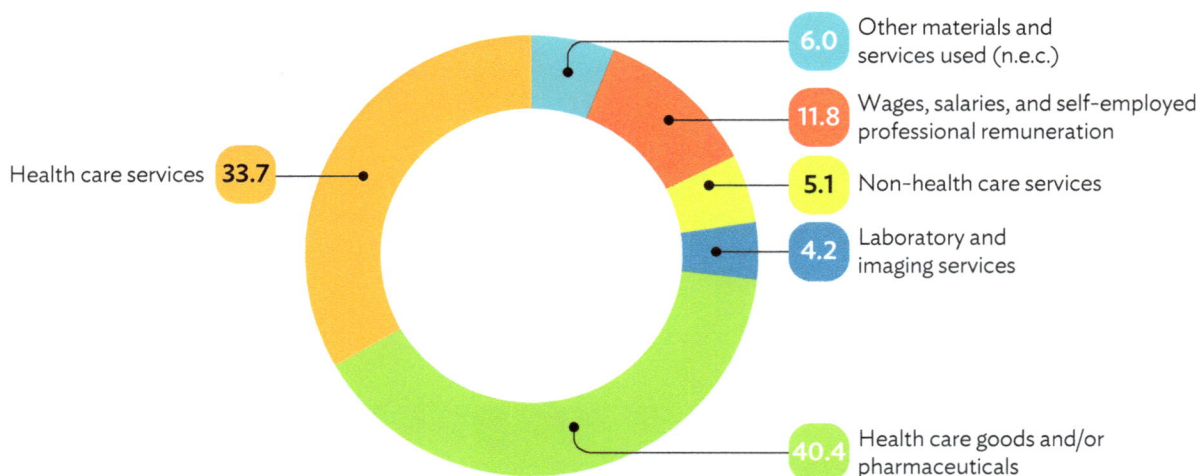

- Other materials and services used (n.e.c.) — 6.0
- Wages, salaries, and self-employed professional remuneration — 11.8
- Non-health care services — 5.1
- Laboratory and imaging services — 4.2
- Health care goods and/or pharmaceuticals — 40.4
- Health care services — 33.7

Source: National Health Accounts 2017–2018, Ministry of Health and Population.

As previously discussed, OOPS is the primary source of funding for Nepal's health care system. This highlights the financial strain placed on families in order to access health care services. The majority of household OOPS was spent on purchasing medicines and medical products from retailers, as well as on health care services for noncommunicable diseases. Notably, the burden of purchasing medicines was significantly higher for poorer households compared to the wealthiest households.

In 2011, the cumulative incidence rate of catastrophic health expenditure was 10.3% per month in Nepal. Households were classified as having catastrophic health expenditure when their OOPS was greater than or equal to 40% of their capacity to pay. Catastrophic health expenditure was concentrated in the poorer quintiles and in Sudurpaschim. Furthermore, this study demonstrated that increased illness episodes in a household triggered catastrophic health expenditure. Catastrophic health expenditure was also influenced by a household's regional location, economic status, chronic illness, acute illness, and education of household head. Findings of this study underscored the importance of incorporating efforts to effectively prioritize the vulnerable households and improve literacy with the current endeavors of the Government of Nepal (Ghimire et al. 2018).

OVERVIEW OF THE NATIONAL HEALTH INSURANCE PROGRAM

The health insurance program's design follows a typical approach used by low- and middle-income countries transitioning away from user fees. The NHIP receives financial contributions from both the Government of Nepal and its members in the form of insurance premiums. Membership must be renewed annually. The current annual premium is NRs3,500 ($26.40) per family, with an additional NRs700 ($5.30) fee for each additional insured member beyond five family members. The government provides subsidies on the premiums for certain targeted groups: ultra-poor, senior citizens, severely disabled, leprosy patients, multidrug-resistant tuberculosis patients, and HIV/AIDS patient households receive a full subsidy.[2] The government provides 50% subsidy on premiums of female community health volunteers. To identify poor households, the health insurance schemes rely on the poverty card issued by the Ministry of Cooperatives and Poverty Alleviation. Enrollment assistants visit households to facilitate enrollment, and they receive a commission of NRs250 ($1.90) for each family they enroll using a mobile app (HIB 2021).

Members of NHIP are entitled to free care at empaneled health facilities up to a maximum of NRs100,000 ($754) per family annually. Families with more than five members receive an additional benefit of NRs20,000 ($150.80) for each additional member, not exceeding a maximum benefit ceiling of NRs200,000 ($1,508.30) per family. The NHIP's benefit package covers emergency services, outpatient consultations, inpatient services, selected medicines, and diagnostic services. Certain services considered unnecessary or too expensive are excluded, such as cosmetic surgery, secondary equipment or machines (such as artificial organs), prescription eyeglasses costing more than NRs500 ($3.80), hearing equipment, services related to artificial insemination, abortion services, dental services, and treatment for injuries resulting from fights or drug or alcohol consumption. Members select their preferred "first service point," typically their nearest primary health care center, which treats them and refers them to secondary care if necessary. Health facilities are reimbursed by case-based payment for outpatients and emergency services and by fee for service for inpatients and diagnostic services. The NHIP is a cashless system, so members receive services and medicines covered by the program without paying at any stage. The health insurance scheme pays providers based on claims submitted through openIMIS,[3] with payments made according to agreed upon rates. Refer to Table 8 for key features of the health insurance scheme (HIB 2022).

---

[2]   Ultra-poor citizens are those bearing poverty cards issued by the Ministry of Land Management, Cooperatives, and Poverty Alleviation senior citizens over 70 years, and people with identity cards of severe disability.

[3]   OpenIMIS is an internet-based open-source software that enables sharing of data among health financing and social protection scheme beneficiaries, providers, and payers.

Table 8: Key Features of the Health Insurance Scheme in Nepal

Characteristics	Key Features
Provider purchaser split	Health Insurance Act has made HIB autonomous
Revenue source	Budget allocated by Government of Nepal and insurance premiums
Enrollment	Mandatory for all by the Health Insurance Act
Subsidy	To defined target groups[a]
Contribution	NRs3,500 ($26.40) for a five-member family/year NRs700 ($5.30) per additional member
Benefit	NRs100,000 ($754.00) for up to five family members, NRs20,000 ($150.80) additional per family member not exceeding NRs200,000 ($1,508.30).
Co-payment	Yes[b]
Services covered	Outpatient, emergency, inpatient, medicines, laboratory and diagnostics, and added transportation for emergency only
Service delivery sites	Accredited public and private facilities
Gatekeeping	Primary health care centers/nearest public health facility
Provider payment mechanism	Fee for service and diagnostics
Information management	OpenIMIS used for registration of membership, renewal, claim management and reporting
Claim management	Health facilities submit claims to HIB through openIMIS HIB reviews and approves claims

HIB = Health Insurance Board, MOHP = Ministry of Health and Population.
[a]   The Government of Nepal provides 100% subsidies on the premiums for certain targeted groups: ultra-poor households, senior citizens over 70 years, severely disabled citizens, leprosy patients, multidrug-resistant tuberculosis patients, and HIV/AIDS patient households. The government also provides 50% subsidy on premiums of female community health volunteers.
[b]   The HIB implemented a co-payment mechanism in December 2023. Under this system, service users are required to pay 10% of the total medical expenses at the point of every health service use. However, patients from targeted groups, as well as service users at primary health care centers and hospitals below 25 beds, are exempted from the co-payment requirement.
Source: HIB 2021.

Payment to service providers is made based on a package of services provided by the HIB. The current benefits package which has been in effect since the inception of the NHIP in 2017 includes 152 types of laboratory tests, 72 types of imaging services (radiology and others), 102 types of medical procedures, 36 types of cardiac treatment procedures, 915 types of surgical treatment procedures, and medical supplies used in 43 types of surgeries. Additionally, the system provides access to 1,133 types of allopathic medicines and medical supplies, as well as 25 types of Ayurvedic and alternative medicines (HIB 2022).

Enrollment Mechanism

Enrollment assistants, based in wards at each local level, are responsible for recruiting individual households into the health insurance scheme. They gather information concerning household members, which is later verified by enrollment officers typically located at the district level. Upon successful verification, individuals receive insurance cards, officially becoming members of the health insurance program. Generally, newly enrolled members can only begin utilizing health services 3 months after enrollment. Membership remains effective for 1 year, with the option for annual renewals (HIB 2023).

Management of Fraud, Waste, and Abuse

Management of fraud, waste, and abuse has been mainly done through HIB's grievance handling section (HIB 2022). Although a separate section at HIB to manage fraud, waste, and abuse is not fully functional at HIB, the draft health insurance road map outlines the HIB's strategy to address these issues.[4] The draft road map has included provisions to warn, penalize, and remove service providers making fraudulent claims as needed.

    (i)   Provide a warning for listed health service providers committing errors once in each quarter.

    (ii)   Impose a penalty for those committing errors twice in each quarter.

    (iii)   Remove from the list those committing errors three times or more in each quarter or as specified.

Moreover, the draft road map focuses on warning, suspension, and dismissal of HIB employees responsible for erroneous claim examination, claim verification, and payment as per the board's decision. This includes financial penalties and prosecution for embezzled amounts (MOHP 2023).

Governance and Budgeting

The Health Insurance Act 2017 establishes the HIB as an autonomous body at the federal level, responsible for managing the health insurance scheme in Nepal. The board of HIB is comprised of nine members including an individual appointed as chair by the Government of Nepal, and another government appointee to serve as board executive director, one member (joint secretary level) nominated by the Ministry of Health and Population (MOHP), one member (joint secretary level) from the Ministry of Finance, three experts nominated by MOHP as members, and two NHIP enrollees, including one female nominated by MOHP (HIB 2022). HIB has a decentralized organization structure with offices at the federal, provincial, and district level undertaking tasks related to administration, planning, training, grievance management, monitoring and evaluation,

---

[4]   The MOHP took the lead in preparing the health insurance program strategic road map 2024–2030. The draft road map was developed and submitted to the Minister of Health to address the gaps in health insurance implementation, leverage political and policy commitment; and achieve significant improvements in health service access, quality, and financial protection.

claims processing and payment, and information management. At the federal or central office level, HIB consists of 42 staff, including 31 permanent staff and 11 on temporary appointment (HIB 2021). At the provincial level, there are 15 staff, including 8 provincial coordinators and 7 office clerks. At the district level, there are 305 registration officers and 5,982 registration assistants, with 1 registration assistant in each ward (HIB 2021).

As shown in Figure 6, the HIB's expenditure has exhibited a consistent upward trajectory over the past seven fiscal years, reflecting a notable increase in the Government of Nepal's financial commitments toward NHIP. Starting at NRs1,359 million in FY2017/2018, the expenditure more than doubled by the end of FY2018/2019 fiscal year, reaching NRs2,770 million. Subsequent fiscal years witnessed substantial growth, with expenditures rising to NRs4,653 million in FY2019/2020 and NRs7,361 million in FY2020/2021. The highest point in the expenditure trend was observed in FY2022/2023, where the HIB allocated a substantial NRs8,736 million. However, the subsequent budget allocation was decreased to NRs7,500 million in FY2023/2024.

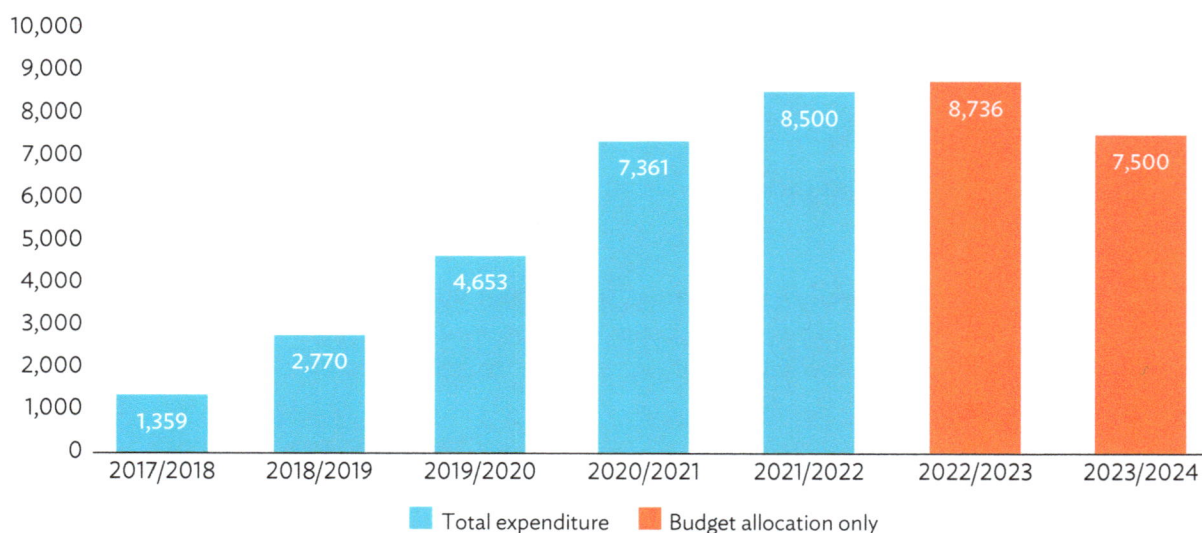

Figure 6: Trends in Budget Expenditure
(NRs million)

Source: Analysis of Red Book FY2017/2018-FY2023/2024, Ministry of Finance.

As shown in Figure 7, the major budget headings under health insurance include reimbursements to empaneled health facilities, payment of premiums to target population, and human resources and capacity building. The allocation for the three major budget items has been increasing. For instance, NRs1.03 billion went to payment of claims to empaneled hospitals, NRs513 million to premium payments of specified population, and NRs257 million to human resources and capacity building in FY2017/2018; these amounts were NRs4.82 billion for claims payment, NRs2 billion for premium payments, and NRs544 million for capacity building in FY2020/2021. In contrast, budget allocation toward other administration costs (including awareness raising) has been decreasing, though it slightly increased in FY2018/2019 and FY2019/2020. In FY2018/2019, empaneled health facilities from Bagmati received the highest share of the total allocation for claims reimbursements at 35.79%, whereas Madhesh (0.30 %), Sudurpaschim (2.5 %), and Karnali (4.51 %) received the lowest shares.

Figure 7: Trends in Budget Allocation by Activities
(NRs '000)

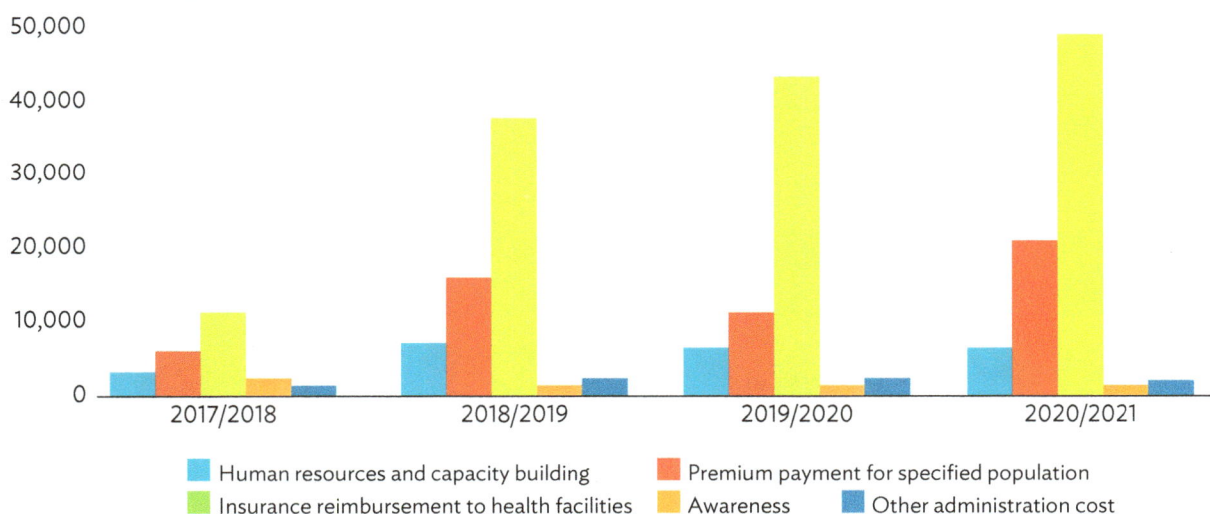

Legend:
- Human resources and capacity building
- Insurance reimbursement to health facilities
- Premium payment for specified population
- Awareness
- Other administration cost

Source: Analysis of Red Book FY2017/18-FY2020/21, Ministry of Finance.

Program Coverage

By the end of 2022, the health insurance program had been rolled out in 77 districts and 746 of the total 753 local government levels (HIB 2022), a gradual process of expansion that began in 2015 when the program was implemented in a single district (Figure 8).[5] During the same period, the population coverage stood at 5,967,408 (22.5% of national population) and total families covered were 1,832,105 (33.7% of total families). Of the total population covered, 3,383,614 (57%)

---

[5]   Districts constitute one of administrative divisions in Nepal. There are altogether 77 districts. Nepal is governed by three tiers of governments: federal government, seven provincial governments, and 753 local government levels.

renewed their membership (Figure 9). Among all population registered, 2,427,089 (40.7%) members used health insurance scheme services. HIB had reimbursed more than NRs21 billion to the empaneled facilities by the end of 2022 (HIB 2022).

Figure 8: Health Insurance Scheme Expansion across Districts of Nepal

New Districts	Year	Cumulative Districts
1	2015	1
7	2016	8
24	2017	32
10	2018	42
14	2019	56
19	2020	75
2	2022	77

● New Districts   ● Cumulative Districts

Source: Health Insurance Board, 2022.

Figure 9: Major Indicators of Health Insurance Scheme

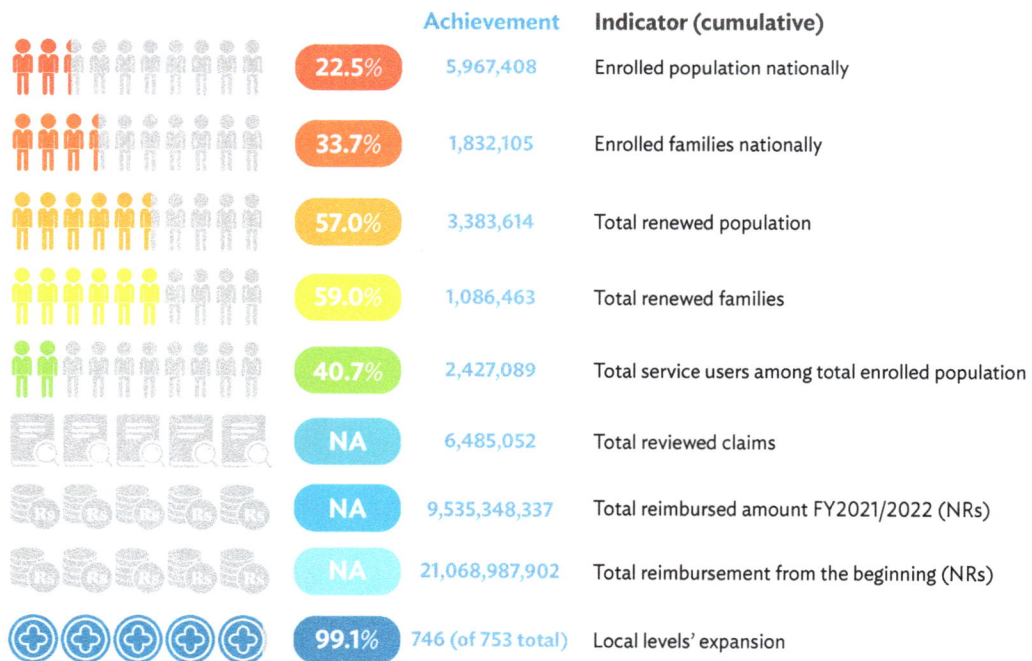

	Achievement		Indicator (cumulative)
	22.5%	5,967,408	Enrolled population nationally
	33.7%	1,832,105	Enrolled families nationally
	57.0%	3,383,614	Total renewed population
	59.0%	1,086,463	Total renewed families
	40.7%	2,427,089	Total service users among total enrolled population
	NA	6,485,052	Total reviewed claims
	NA	9,535,348,337	Total reimbursed amount FY2021/2022 (NRs)
	NA	21,068,987,902	Total reimbursement from the beginning (NRs)
	99.1%	746 (of 753 total)	Local levels' expansion

FY = fiscal year, NRs = Nepalese rupees.
Source: Health Insurance Board, 2022.

Koshi has the highest program coverage among all provinces in Nepal, with 42% of its total population covered by health insurance. In contrast, Madhesh has the lowest NHIP coverage, where only 8% of its population has health insurance (Figure 10). Sudurpaschim has the highest number of its targeted population enrolled in NHIP, at 279,085 members. Meanwhile, Madhesh (at 137,912 members) and Karnali (at 129,703 members) have the lowest number of its targeted population groups enrolled in NHIP (Table 9). A field study was conducted in Koshi, Madhesh, and Gandaki provinces to understand the contributing factors to these provincial differences in health insurance scheme coverage.

Figure 10: Population Coverage by Province

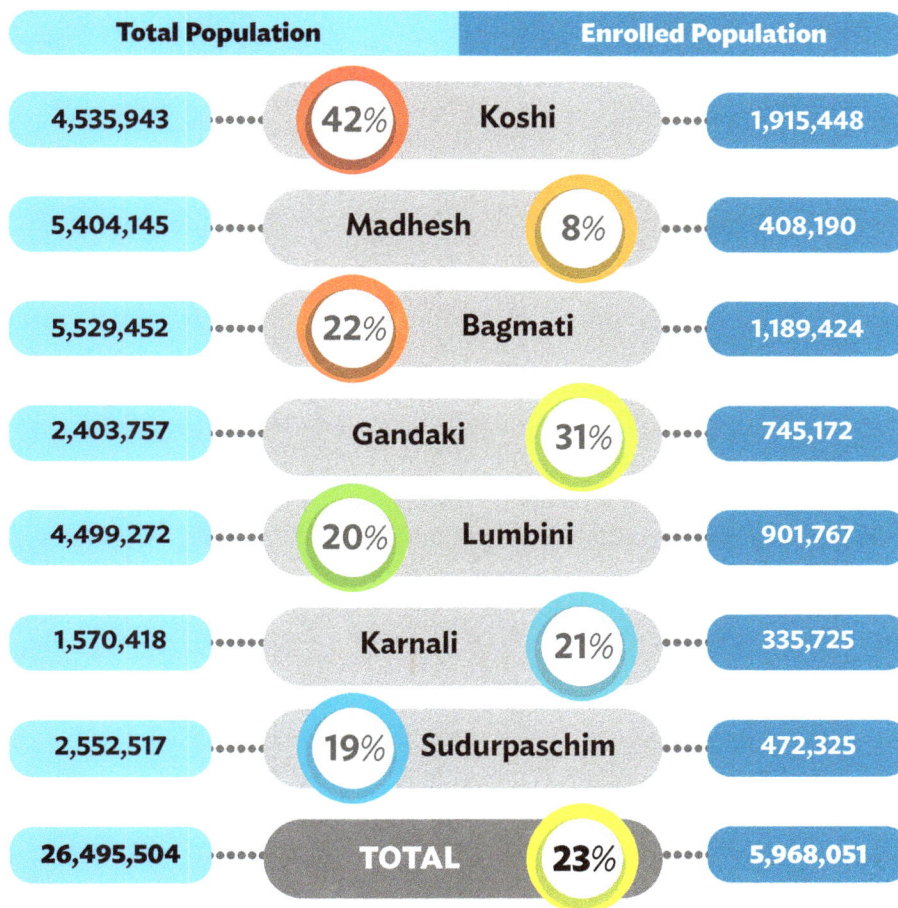

Total Population		Enrolled Population
4,535,943	42% Koshi	1,915,448
5,404,145	Madhesh 8%	408,190
5,529,452	22% Bagmati	1,189,424
2,403,757	Gandaki 31%	745,172
4,499,272	20% Lumbini	901,767
1,570,418	Karnali 21%	335,725
2,552,517	19% Sudurpaschim	472,325
26,495,504	TOTAL 23%	5,968,051

Source: Health Insurance Board, 2022.

Table 9: Enrollment of General and Targeted Population by Province

Province	Estimated Population	General Enrolled Population	Targeted Enrolled Population	Total Enrolled Population	%
Koshi	4,535,943	1,638,505	276,943	1,915,448	42
Madhesh	5,404,145	270,278	137,912	408,190	8
Bagmati	5,529,452	1,017,166	172,258	1,189,424	22
Gandaki	2,403,757	573,304	171,868	745,172	31
Lumbini	4,499,272	624,254	277,513	901,767	20
Karnali	1,570,418	206,022	129,703	335,725	21
Sudurpaschim	2,552,517	193,240	279,085	472,325	19
Total	**26,495,504**	**4,522,769**	**1,445,282**	**5,968,051**	**23**

Source: Health Insurance Board, 2022.

As highlighted in Box 2, a higher awareness level; the presence of higher numbers of empaneled facilities; and the availability of health services, medicines, and health care providers were some of the key factors contributing to the higher NHIP coverage in Koshi compared to Madhesh and Gandaki.

Over 40% of the enrolled population in Karnali dropped out of NHIP, more than 10 percentage points than the national average of 29%. This is also the highest dropout rate for the health insurance program among provinces in Nepal (for comparison, Bagmati and Sudurpaschim had the lowest dropout rate at 27%) (Table 10). It is particularly interesting to note that only 30% of Karnali's local government levels have empaneled facilities, the lowest among provinces. On the other hand, Koshi has the highest number of empaneled facilities in Nepal, with 62% of its local government levels having at least one empaneled health facility (Table 11). Among the enrolled population, 47% in Bagmati utilized health care services, followed by 44% in Koshi and 42% in Gandaki (Table 10) (HIB 2022).

Table 10: Total Enrolled, Dropout, and Service Utilization by Province
(Cumulative)

Province	Total Enrolled	Total Dropout	% of Dropout	Total Enrolled Population with Service Utilization	% of Enrolled Population with Service Utilization
Koshi	1,915,448	573,872	30	846,957	44
Madhesh	408,190	96,407	24	100,463	25
Bagmati	1,189,424	323,460	27	559,350	47
Gandaki	745,172	217,495	29	311,927	42
Lumbini	901,767	248,293	28	348,263	39
Karnali	335,725	138,405	41	125,170	37
Sudurpaschim	472,325	125,318	27	134,536	28
Total	**5,968,051**	**1,723,250**	**29**	**2,426,666**	**41**

Source: Health Insurance Board, 2022.

Box 2: Understanding Factors Influencing Coverage of Health Insurance Scheme in Koshi, Madhesh, and Gandaki

This is a summary of the field study conducted to investigate the factors affecting differences in health insurance scheme coverage in three provinces: Koshi, Madhesh, and Gandaki. One of the themes that emerged is the awareness of the health insurance scheme, which was identified as a key factor in enrolling people; a majority of insured members in Koshi mentioned several benefits of the program including protection from financial hardships during health emergencies. However, in Madhesh, people seemed to be less aware of the program, and this was cited as one of the major reasons for low enrollment in this province.

> **Pokhara, Nepal.** People queuing in a National Health Insurance Program dedicated counter at Pokhara Academy of Health Science hospital (photo by Rakesh Ayer).

"People lack awareness of the benefits of health insurance. They also don't know where and how to seek service after getting enrolled in the program. There is high illiteracy present in this municipality. It could be the main reason why people have not enrolled." Community health unit supervisor, Bhangaha Municipality.

The management of the health insurance scheme was another theme that emerged from the interviews, with some insured members being unaware of their membership expiry and renewal dates, and the insurance card being of low quality. Issues were also raised regarding the overutilization of health services as an insured member.

"I didn't know my insurance my expired. I only came to know about it when I went to the hospital for my health checkup and I couldn't get it done. I thought my membership was still valid. I was confused when my renewal date was and could not get renewed on time. If there was a provision to know renewal date in advance, I would have renewed it on time and received health services." Insured member Janakpur, Madhesh.

The availability and quality of services were also identified as themes that affect health insurance scheme coverage. In Madhesh and Gandaki, the availability of empaneled health facilities was limited, and the quality of services provided was inadequate. These were cited as reasons for low enrollment and dissatisfaction among insured members in these provinces. Governance and engagement of local and provincial governments in health insurance scheme implementation were also identified as themes, with the lack of coordination and communication among stakeholders cited as major challenges.

"We have to spend long time waiting to see the doctor. Before being enrolled in health insurance, I didn't spend as long time as these days. There should be more staff at the hospital to look after insured members." Insured member, Pokhara, Gandaki.

"Whenever I go to hospital to seek care, I don't get all the prescribed medicines. What do I do if we do not get medicine? Even basic medicines are not available sometimes. This is even after standing in the long queue for more than hour." Insured member, Saptari, Madhesh.

Source: Findings from in-depth interviews conducted in Koshi, Madhesh, and Gandaki Provinces

Table 11: Local-Level Governments by the Presence of Listed Health Service Providers

Province	Total Local Levels	Local Levels Covered by the Empaneled Service Providers	% of Local Levels with Empaneled Facilities
Koshi	137	85	62
Madhesh	136	50	37
Bagmati	119	58	49
Gandaki	85	40	47
Lumbini	109	54	50
Karnali	79	24	30
Sudurpaschim	88	32	36
Total	**753**	**343**	**46**

Source: Health Insurance Board, 2022.

More than 80% of the empaneled health facilities are public hospitals and primary health care centers (PHCCs). Of the total 189 PHCCs in Nepal, 186 are empaneled. Only about 11% (48) of the total (452) are community-based or private hospitals, while 6.2% (28) are eye hospitals (Table 12).

1. The percentage of enrolled population from Karnali and Sudurpaschim provinces is similar to that of Bagmati and Gandaki provinces (Table 9), despite low health service indicators among populations in Karnali and Sudurpaschim. This suggests that people in these provinces may have better access to services. However, Karnali and Sudurpaschim also have the highest proportion of people in the poorest wealth quintile (65.9% for Karnali and 40.6% for Sudurpaschim) (Table 3). Moreover, the proportion of insured people on average remains below 25% nationally, indicating challenges with enrollment and re-enrollment.

Table 12: Distribution of Empaneled Health Facilities by Type and Province

Province	Public Hospital	Primary Health Care Center	Community/ Private Hospital	Eye Hospital	Total
Koshi	44	40	19	7	110
Madhesh	16	34	8	5	63
Bagmati	51	30	8	6	95
Gandaki	24	24	4	1	53
Lumbini	23	28	5	6	62
Karnali	16	14	1	2	33
Sudurpaschim	16	16	3	1	36
Total	**190**	**186**	**48**	**28**	**452**

Source: Health Insurance Board, 2022.

2. Also, the majority of the local government levels (410 of 753) in Nepal do not have any empaneled health facility. A total of 452 health facilities are empaneled to provide health services under the NHIP across 343 local government levels in Nepal. Koshi has the highest number of empaneled health facilities among all the provinces; of its 137 local levels, 85 (62%) have empaneled health facilities. Conversely, Karnali (30%), Madhesh (37%), and Sudurpaschim (36%) have the lowest number of NHIP-registered health facilities across their respective local government levels (Table 11).

3. As highlighted in Box 3, the key bottlenecks toward the successful implementation of health insurance scheme are low enrollment rates, limited institutional capacity of HIB, and lack of revision of benefits package. These challenges were reported during the consultations with stakeholders such as public health care providers, policymakers at national and subnational levels, professional councils, professional associations, development partners, and the private sector.

Box 3: Stakeholders' Perspectives

The implementation of the National Health Insurance Program has been highlighted as an issue due to low enrollment rates, and stakeholders have pointed out that there has been insufficient attention given to assessing factors contributing to enrollment, re-enrollment, and dropout rates. Institutional capacity of the Health Insurance Board is also limited, leading to delays in processing claims and difficulty in service delivery, with stakeholders suggesting an assessment of current capacity to improve efficiency. It is also noted that a sufficiently healthy pool of members is necessary for any insurance scheme to survive, and a bottleneck analysis may be useful in identifying difficulties in implementing mandatory enrollment of population subgroups. Additionally, the benefit package design has been criticized for including services already covered by free care programs, and stakeholders suggest grouping together programs with elements of social protection under one umbrella.

Stakeholders from the private sector have highlighted the lack of a standard behavior change communication strategy for promoting enrollment in the health insurance program and recommended assessing the effectiveness of current methods and developing more appropriate ones. The success of the health insurance scheme will depend largely on its ability to provide financial protection to poor people and marginalized groups, but there is no agreed methodology or standards for defining who are poor people. Stakeholders from the academic sector suggest undertaking a scientific costing of services to determine the reimbursement of disease, drugs, and conditions before the cost becomes expensive.

The impacts of the health insurance scheme on financial protection and the population's health and well-being given the current benefit package have been discussed, with stakeholders suggesting that evidence is needed to inform changes to scheme design, such as the benefit package and purchasing arrangements. Additionally, stakeholders have raised concerns about the lack of incentive for insured individuals to remain healthy, with private facilities riding on the out-of-pocket expenses by encouraging patients to use their annual benefits for general check-ups, thus exhausting balances for catastrophic illnesses.

Source: Findings from the field study.

Claims Management

The claim reimbursement process is a structured and multi-layered system designed to ensure accuracy and adherence to HIB policies. Initially, service providers lodge claims using the OpenIMIS via an application programming interface or API. Once submitted, the OpenIMIS automatically reviews these claims against HIB policy filters, which may lead to the rejection of certain services or the entire claim if discrepancies are found. Claims that pass this initial stage reach the claims management department, where specialized personnel meticulously review the submitted claims alongside the uploaded documents. In some cases, the department may request additional supporting documentation to further substantiate the claim before granting approval for reimbursement. Claims that remain unresolved are referred to a dedicated committee for quality control and monitoring, assessing the intricacies of each case to ensure fairness and compliance with set standards. The information technology department then generates detailed statements for the approved claims, which are subjected to a final review through the executive director of HIB verification. Once cleared, the claims are routed to the accounts section, where the payment release process is finalized (HIB 2023).

Claims management at HIB employs a dedicated team of 20 staff, including medical officers, pharmacy officers, nursing officers, and medical lab officers that handle between 25,000 to 30,000 claims received daily from various health service providers. Despite this high volume, the staff's manual review capacity peaks at only 5,500 to 6,500 claims per day. The procedural mandate requires claims to be filled within 7 days and supporting documents within 15 days, yet the absence of a live claim review system often leads to process delays (HIB 2023). Adherence to the 2021 settlement guidelines is ensured through a method of random sampling for claim settlements (HIB 2023).

Claims submitted are examined and verified by the claims management section at the HIB. Claims up to NRs500 are approved without further scrutiny, while claims ranging from NRs501 to NRs5,000 undergo a 10% random sampling evaluation. Additionally, a system is in place to assess all claims exceeding NRs5,000 (HIB 2023).

Figure 11 shows the total claim amount received by the HIB from FY2016 to FY2022. The y-axis shows the total claim amount received in NRs. The x-axis shows the fiscal year. The data shows an upward trend in the total claim amount received by the HIB over the past seven fiscal years. The total claimed amount received increased from NRs2,391,003 in 2016 to NRs13,708,666,305 in 2022. This is an increase of 13.7 billion.

Figure 12 shows the trend in claims received by HIB in the last seven fiscal years. The number of claims received by HIB has been significantly increasing in recent years. The total claims received in 2022 was over 7 million, compared to about 4,000 claims during the start of HIB in 2016.

The prevailing prescription management is paper-based and manual. The HIB offers uniform benefit packages across all health facilities, but these packages do not cover all services and items, and there is no capping system in place for government programs. Pricing is managed via a predetermined price list for certain services and items, with benefit packages that bundle lab tests, medicines, and procedures together. However, exclusions within the benefit packages are notable, with certain services such as cosmetic surgery, certain high-cost equipment, artificial insemination, organ transplants, sex transformation procedures, and some aspects of dental care not being covered (HIB 2023).

Figure 11: Trend in Claims Amount Received by Health Insurance Board (NRs billion)

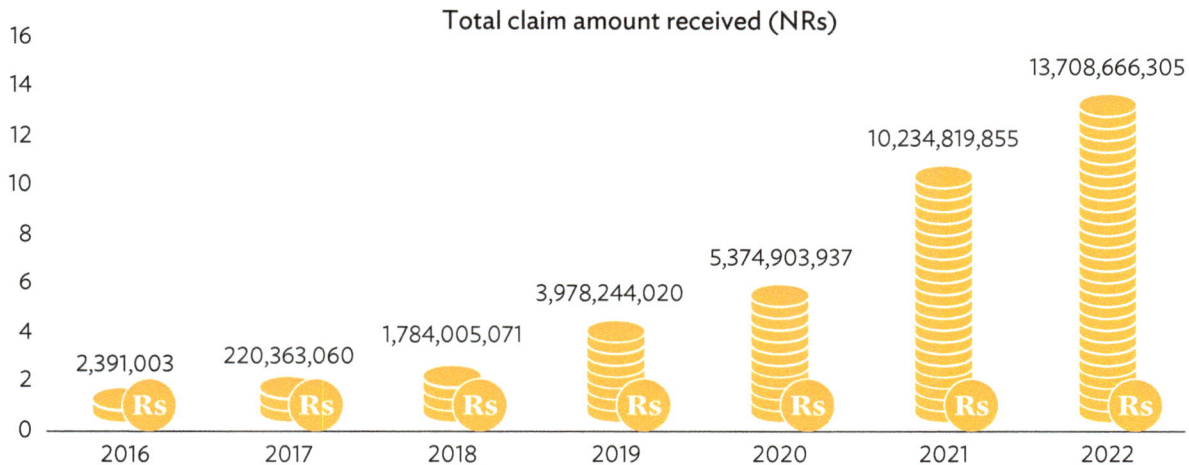

Total claim amount received (NRs)

Year	Total claim amount received (NRs)
2016	2,391,003
2017	220,363,060
2018	1,784,005,071
2019	3,978,244,020
2020	5,374,903,937
2021	10,234,819,855
2022	13,708,666,305

Source: Health Insurance Board, 2023.

Figure 12: Trend in Number of Claims per Year Received by Health Insurance Board (million)

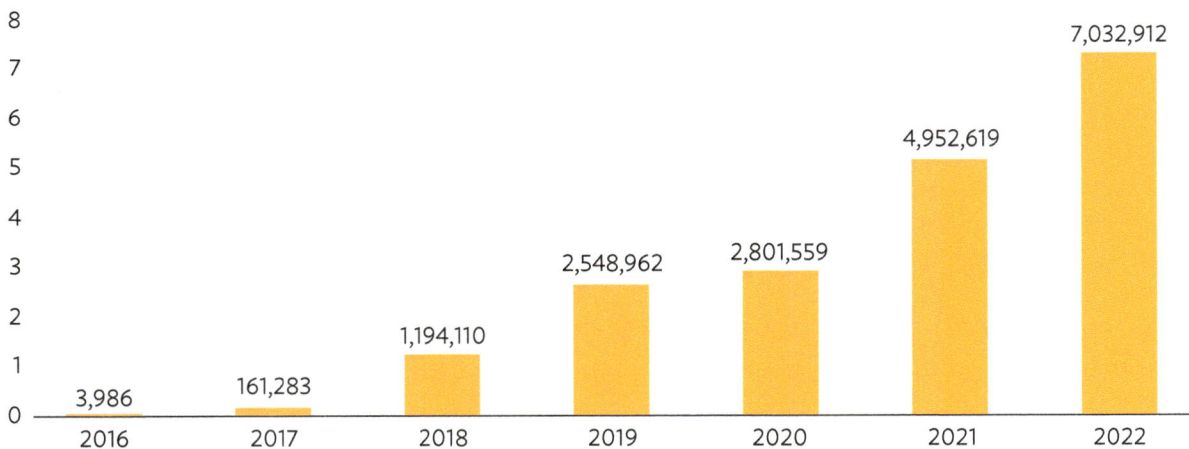

Year	Number of claims
2016	3,986
2017	161,283
2018	1,194,110
2019	2,548,962
2020	2,801,559
2021	4,952,619
2022	7,032,912

Source: Health Insurance Board, 2023.

The claims management process faces several challenges that undermine its efficiency and reliability. Foremost among these is the slow pace of claim settlements, with a significant backlog in the settlement and reimbursement of claims, which frustrates all stakeholders involved. The task of ensuring the rational use of diagnoses and drug prescriptions further complicates the process, since the current staff complement lacks the expertise required for such a task. There have also been cases of improper handling of referral claims, e.g., dual claims that escape verification checks, as well as the increasing instances of fraud, abuse, and waste, with inadequate human resources and outdated software unable to detect and prevent deceitful practices. To add, the claims management department still have to monitor and evaluate the top 25 health facilities, where only half the reimbursements are effectively supervised. Ultimately, ambiguous ownership of work responsibilities within the HIB aggravates these claims-related issues (HIB 2023).

Benefit Package

With the implementation of NHIP, the HIB introduced its benefit package in 2017 aimed at providing comprehensive health care coverage to its beneficiaries. The HIB's benefit package was originally formulated using an input-based approach, which involved collecting and assessing a list of services and their associated costs. These services were then categorized into various components, including laboratory tests, radiological and other diagnostic services, medical packages, surgical packages, cancer care-related services, cardiac care-related packages, allopathic medicines, Ayurvedic medicines, and surgical items and consumables. The average rate of each service was established, forming the basis of the benefit package. Payments to service providers were made based on the services included in the health insurance benefit package (HIB 2023).

The package encompasses 152 types of laboratory tests, 72 types of imaging services (radiology and others), 102 types of medical treatment procedures, 36 types of heart-related treatment procedures, and 915 types of surgical services, in addition to various materials used in 43 types of surgeries. Provision is also made for the reimbursement of services not covered by the mentioned treatment methods and procedures, based on claims submitted by health service providers. The benefit package also incorporates arrangements for 1,133 types of modern medical services and related medicines and materials, as well as 25 types of Ayurvedic and alternative medicines (HIB 2022).

The price list for various medical procedures, including laboratory tests, radiological and other diagnostic services, medical and surgical packages, as well as medicines, was first collected from various public hospitals and health centers. Subsequently, the HIB conducted a workshop with all concerned experts such as physicians specializing in various medical fields. The prices of different services were averaged and subsequently incorporated into the benefit package (HIB 2023).

Recognizing the need for periodic updates and adjustments to align with evolving health care needs and costs, the HIB conducted a partial revision of its benefit package in 2021. This revision primarily focused on the rates of services and medicines within the package. Specifically, rates for 104 services, including medical packages, surgical packages, radiological investigations, and undefined services from the "others" category were revised. Additionally, the rates of 69 medicines were also updated (HIB 2023).

HIB initiated a comprehensive revision of the benefit package in May 2023, with the primary objective of enhancing the existing benefit package through an input-based and analytical approach. The subsequent sections discuss various aspects of this revision process, including categorization, verification, rate determination, and customization. It also addresses the challenges faced during this process and outlines strategies to overcome them. Four steps were undertaken to categorize the current benefit package:

(i)   **Collection of service lists and rates.** The initial phase of the revision process involved meticulously listing the services included in the existing benefit package and collecting their corresponding rates. This comprehensive data collection was essential for the subsequent phases of the revision.

(ii)   **Verification of list of services and addition of missing services.** To ensure the accuracy and completeness of the list of services, a thorough verification process was conducted. Any missing services were identified and added to the package during this phase, ensuring that beneficiaries receive a comprehensive package.

(iii)   **Addition of verified services to defined categories.** The services were categorized based on their nature and purpose. This categorization is vital for streamlining coverage and ensuring that beneficiaries can easily understand and access the services they need.

(iv)   **Calculation of weighted average and mode value from rates collected.** The rates collected were used to calculate both the weighted average and mode values. These calculations are crucial for rate determination, as they provide insights into the distribution of costs among different services, helping to set appropriate rates.

The micro-costing approach was adopted to determine the rates for each service, particularly for surgical packages. The total rate for surgical procedures was calculated as the sum of several components, including anesthesia charges; laboratory, radiology, and physiotherapy charges; procedure charges; consumables charges; and medicines charges. For medicines, market assessments were conducted, and the average rate was calculated. A standard practice by the Department of Drug Administration involved reducing the calculated average maximum retail price of each medicine by 15% (HIB 2023).

a. Benefit Package Customization

HIB adopted two approaches to customize the benefit package: first, by categorizing the benefit package by health facility types, and second, by implementing a co-payment mechanism.

(i)   **Health facility types.** The revised benefit package will be classified into five different categories based on the type of health facility. These categories will include up to 15 bedded hospitals, 25–30 bedded hospitals, 100–500 bedded hospitals, specialty hospitals, and specialized hospitals. This categorization allows for tailored coverage based on the capacity and specialization of the health care providers, ensuring that beneficiaries receive appropriate care.

(ii)   **Co-payment.** A significant addition to the revised benefit package is the implementation of a co-payment method. This method involves beneficiaries sharing a portion of the health care costs. The co-payment guidelines outline when and to what extent co-payment applies, categorizing services and service providers for clarity. A 10% co-payment mechanism was implemented from December 2023 (HIB 2023).

b. Challenges Faced by Health Insurance Board in Benefit Package Revision

The HIB has faced four major challenges in benefit package revisions:

(i) **Payment method and benefit design.** One of the major challenges faced during the revision process was the rapid nationwide rollout of the current benefit package. This rollout occurred without adequate time for pre-testing or piloting, leading to a hastily finalized package. The reliance on a fee-for-service payment method without a thorough assessment of its cost-effectiveness has raised concerns. Moreover, dependence on service provider rates has further complicated the design.

(ii) **Resource constraints.** A critical challenge in benefit package revision has been the lack of experts to guide the process. This has resulted in gaps in coverage for essential treatments, medicines, and services. Furthermore, assessing the financial implications of the package has been challenging due to resource constraints, hindering the development of a truly cost-effective package.

(iii) **Changing health care landscape.** The evolving health care landscape has introduced complexities to the benefit package. Rapid advancements in medical technologies, treatment modalities, market rates, and pharmaceuticals, coupled with a high disease burden, demand ongoing adaptation. Additionally, regulatory changes and policy reforms necessitate careful consideration, which the current package did not accommodate.

(iv) **Lack of standard treatment guidelines and rates.** Significant variations in rates exist, even among government hospitals, for investigations, services, administrative processes, and medicines. The absence of price rate caps for health care services and the lack of standardized medicines pricing have compounded these challenges.

Listing and Delisting of Health Facilities

The Guidelines on Listing of Service Providing Institutions, 2021 have been issued by the HIB under the authority granted by Section 41 of the Health Insurance Act, 2017. The aim is to facilitate easy, accessible, organized, and effective service procurement through the listing of service providing institutions within the health insurance program. This is in line with the mandate to monitor, regulate, and evaluate health institutions' service delivery, as outlined in Section 15 (f) of the Health Insurance Act.

As per the guidelines, the following criteria must be fulfilled by health institutions for them to be listed in the HIB:

(i) Application submission with required documents, including institution registration certificate, memorandum of association, articles of association, permanent account number certificate, tax clearance certificate, social security fund participation certificate, service operation license, and other necessary documents.

(ii)   Recommendation letter from the local or provincial health insurance coordination committee.

(iii)   Self-assessment report demonstrating at least 60% score within the minimum service standards set for health institutions by MOHP.

(iv)   Submission of bank statements for staff salary accounts and health insurance documents.

(v)   Documentation or a letter confirming the operation of the service provider's pharmacy.

(vi)   Documentation or a letter confirming the presence of an electronic medical record system.

(vii)   For nongovernment hospitals, a minimum of 25 beds, including three specialized doctors (physician, general surgeon, and gynecologist).

On-site monitoring is conducted after receiving the full set of documents. Health institutions that achieve at least 60% compliance with minimum service standards are recommended to the board of HIB for potential listing.

There are provisions for delisting health institutions, with the delisting criteria based on the same guidelines cited as follows:

(i)   Once listed, the service providing institutions delivering services must fulfill the standards within 3 months as per the guidelines.

(ii)   Removal from the list and restriction of all payments if irregularities or embezzlements are proven in payment for services delivered.

(iii)   Board discretion to remove service providing institutions if there is a lack of regularity in abiding by prescribed standards.

Listing of the health institutions is also guided by the following miscellaneous criteria:

(i)   Delivery of services to be ensured by prioritizing insured individuals as per Section 10 Subsection (3) of the Health Insurance Act, 2017.

(ii)   The HIB retains the authority to add, eliminate, or revise guidelines as per requirements.

(iii)   Final interpretation of guidelines rests with the HIB in case of any ambiguity.

Policy Environment

NHIP is guided by several regulatory and legal frameworks. In addition to regular updates and revisions of existing policies and procedures, NHIP is directed by various legal documents. The 2015 Constitution of Nepal guarantees the right to health care as the fundamental human right of every citizen. It ensures the provision of health insurance to every citizen to facilitate access to health care. The 2015 Health Policy, formulated by the Government of Nepal, is dedicated to ensuring universal access to basic health services free of cost through the establishment of "basic health service facilities" in every ward of the 753 local governments. Moreover, NHIP is also guided by the government's commitment to achieve UHC as part of the SDGs. Target 3.8 of SDGs also emphasizes the importance of implementing a health insurance scheme in Nepal.

Key legal frameworks guiding NHIP include the Health Insurance Act 2017, Public Health Services Act 2018, National Health Policy 2019, National Insurance Policy 2016, Health Insurance Regulations 2018, and the Fifteenth Plan (2019–2023). The Second Long-term Health Plan (1997–2017) aimed to establish community- based health insurance through community-based financing. The Nepal Health Sector Strategy 2015–2022 reinforces the commitment toward ensuring free basic health services (BHS), stating that free BHS and services beyond BHS will be provided at an affordable cost through social health protection arrangements, including targeted subsidies for vulnerable groups. Nepal's commitment to UHC is also evident in the National Health Policy 2014, ensuring free BHS as a fundamental right.

The evolution of NHIP is also shaped by various other health sector strategic frameworks, including the Nepal Health Sector Strategic Plan 2030, National Health Financing Strategy 2033, and Health Insurance Road Map 2030 as drafted by the MOHP in 2023. The First Long-Term Health Plan (1975–1995) emphasized holistic health care, while the 1991 National Health Policy targeted rural health standards through primary health care. The Health Sector Strategy 2004–2009 introduced a sector-wide approach, while the National Health Sector Plan-II (2010–2015) emphasized partnerships, access, equity, and local governance.

The current Nepal Health Sector Strategic Plan 2022–2030 is aligned with the National Health Policy 2019 and aims to achieve health-related SDGs. Integrating with the Fifteenth Plan (2019–2023) and operational until 2030, the health sector strategy intends to improve access to quality health services, address system agendas, and progress toward UHC. The three strategic documents that MOHP drafted in 2023 are also believed to support the effective implementation of NHIP and improve its population coverage. These documents include the Health Insurance Strategic Road Map, Basic Health Services Monitoring Framework, and the National Health Financing Strategy Implementation Plan.

STOCKTAKING OF COMPLETED AND ONGOING STUDIES

As indicated in Table 13, seven of the eight published studies related to health insurance were observational in design. Cross-sectional studies were most commonly used, either using a qualitative approach or a mixed-method approach (qualitative and quantitative). Only one study conducted in 2014 carried out an impact evaluation of the health insurance program in Nepal. However, it only presented baseline findings, since the health insurance scheme was still in its infancy at that time. Additionally, five studies used purposive sampling to select the sample population.

Table 13: List of Studies by Name, Type, and Sampled Population

Name and Year of the Study	Type of Study	Sample Size and Population
Nepal Health Insurance Impact Evaluation: Baseline Basic Report 2014	Impact evaluation based on randomization	7,521 households from six districts
Assessment of Social Health Insurance Scheme in Selected Districts of Nepal 2018	Observational study using mixed-method approach	338 exit client interviews and 54 KIIs in Kailali, Baglung, and Illam districts
Brief Annual Report of HIB FY 2018/2019	An observational study based on desk reviews and secondary analysis	
Factors associated with enrollment of households in Nepal's national health insurance program 2019	Cross-sectional study	570 households from 2 rural municipalities of Illam District
Insuree satisfaction survey and policy research in National Health Insurance Program (NHIP) 2020	Cross-sectional study	1,227 respondents from Jhapa, Palpa, and Kailali districts
Survey Report on Governance Reform of Health Insurance Board 2020	Observational study based on qualitative design	
Status and determinants of enrollment and dropout of health insurance in Nepal: an explorative study 2020	Observational study based on mixed method approach	Enrollment assistants in Bardiya, Chitwan, and Gorkha districts were purposively selected
Awareness on Social Health Insurance Scheme among Locals in Bhaktapur Municipality 2020	Cross-sectional study	Random selection of 385 from 5 different wards of Bhaktapur municipality

FY = fiscal year, HIB = Health Insurance Board, KII = key informant interview, NHIP = National Health Insurance Program.
Source: Authors' findings.

As shown in Table 13, cross-sectional study designs and purposive sampling methods were commonly used in studies related to social health insurance in Nepal. However, it is important to consider that such study designs have limitations and biases. Cross-sectional studies can only provide a snapshot of a situation at a single point in time and cannot be used to analyze behaviors over time, determine cause and effect, or generalize findings if the sample size is too small (Wang and Cheng, 2020). Furthermore, purposive sampling can skew study findings since sample populations are selected deliberately rather than randomly. Despite these limitations, the studies have resulted in findings that are relevant to implementing and expanding health insurance schemes. Appendix 5 details these findings, which are grouped according to name and date of the study, type of study, methods used, sampling frame/sample size, and major findings.

Factors Related to Enrollment and Household Out-of-Pocket Health Spending

The 2022 Nepal Demographic and Health Survey results show that a majority of women (88%) and men (87%) are not enrolled in NHIP. Analyzing the patterns based on background characteristics reveals the following disparities: the coverage is highest in Koshi Province among women (22%) and men (23%) and that women (33%) and men (37%) with more than a secondary education and those in the highest wealth quintile (24% of women and 25% of men) exhibit a higher likelihood of having health insurance compared to their counterparts with no education (5% of women and 3% of men) and those in the lowest wealth quintile (4% of women and 6% of men) (NDHS 2022).

Moreover, similar to NDHS 2022 findings, the cited studies found that people with chronic diseases and better socioeconomic status were more likely to enroll in NHIP. Conversely, HIB has been unable to enroll all people below the extreme poverty line since poverty identification has only taken place in 26 districts of Nepal. This evidence contradicts the risk-pooling mechanism related to health insurance and the objective of achieving UHC when people with chronic diseases are more likely to be insured than healthy individuals and people below the extreme poverty line are less likely to enroll in NHIP.

Similarly, household OOPS regarding outpatient and laboratory services is much lower than for inpatient services and medical supplies. One of the biggest expenses related to outpatient services was transportation to and from health facilities, but the current scheme does not cover these expenses. People, especially in rural parts of Nepal, still have to travel long distances to seek services from health facilities (MOHP, New ERA, and ICF 2017).

Factors Related to Service Delivery

Interviews conducted with NHIP-insured members, enrollment assistants, and respondents from empaneled health facilities in studies presented revealed several challenges related to health care service delivery from empaneled health facilities. First, all medicines listed in the insurance scheme are not available from pharmacies, forcing those insured to pay for medical supplies and seek services from other facilities. It is important to note that the majority of household OOPS were for buying medicines and medical products from retailers (MOHP 2020). This may discourage people from enrolling in NHIP and, most importantly, will not help to reduce the financial risks related to household expenditure on medicines and medical supplies. Second, there are inadequate laboratory services and human resources at empaneled health facilities. Third, the insured face challenges in seeking referral services if these are not available at their preferred health facilities. Fourth, respondents from empaneled health facilities mentioned that the process of getting reimbursed from HIB takes a long time.

Factors Related to Governance and Implementation of the National Health Insurance Program

The absence of an approved permanent structure for the HIB has led to administrative challenges, hindering program effectiveness. To address this, the establishment of a permanent structure for the HIB is deemed essential. The Health Insurance Act and regulations highlight issues arising from the exclusion of the formal sector in NHIP, posing financial challenges to the program. Despite initial enthusiasm among the population, high dropouts in enrollment occur due to citizen dissatisfaction with the health care service quality and reduced renewals.

The current service procurement system lacks a scientific basis, resulting in diagnostic and prescription problems due to undue pressure from service recipients. Because of the lack of poverty identification in all districts, it has been challenging to include the ultra-poor and the marginalized citizens in the program.

Studies have identified several factors related to governance and implementation of NHIP. First, enrollment assistants mentioned the absence of motivation and capacity-building activities to enable them to carry out work effectively. Second, there is lack of integration of programs similar to NHIP and other health insurance schemes that are being implemented in parallel with NHIP. For instance, the Government of Nepal's free BHS is being implemented along with NHIP. In addition, there are other private companies providing schemes related to health insurance. Third, there is a lack of awareness in the community regarding NHIP. This is further aggravated by the decreasing trend in budget allocation toward activities relating to awareness raising.

CONCLUSIONS AND RECOMMENDATIONS

The development of health insurance in Nepal has made progress with the formation of the NHIP, which has been implemented in all provinces and districts. The program is globally acclaimed for financial risk protection in accessing health care and ensures the constitutional mandate to provide health insurance to Nepali citizens. However, government faces several challenges to the program that may hinder achievement of UHC by 2030.

The NHIP's population coverage is currently low at 23%, with notable variations among different provinces. Additionally, there is limited coverage of ultra-poor people; at present ultra-poor citizens of only 26 of the total 77 districts are covered.

The program's risk pooling is limited, with evidence showing that people with chronic illness and higher socioeconomic status are more likely to enroll, potentially compromising its risk pooling mechanism. Program financing has also stagnated in recent years. Nepal's public financing on health at 33% of the CHE is very low, putting further pressure on household spending (current OOPS for health care is high at over 50%). Financial sustainability assessment of the health insurance scheme is also lacking. To add, the program's benefit package has not been updated since its implementation. Attention is required to update the package to ensure the program's fiscal sustainability.

Anecdotal evidence suggests that NHIP implementation may have been hindered by moral hazards, such as fraudulent claims from health service providers and overuse of services by users. The program's impact in terms of providing financial protection is yet to be determined. There are no studies or available data on whether the NHIP has successfully reduced OOPS or not.

Regarding program access, a majority of local-level governments in Nepal still do not have empaneled health facilities, indicating limited access to the NHIP's services among citizens in these areas.

HIB, which is the lead agency in NHIP implementation, needs strengthening through the provision of adequate staffing and automation of claims management to avoid the backlog of claims and ensure efficient health service delivery. There is also limited program ownership across federal, provincial, and local-level governments, reflecting the lack of urgency to improve health outcomes in Nepal.

As discussed, NHIP is essential to the Government of Nepal's goal of achieving UHC by 2030. Despite facing many obstacles, the NHIP has gradually expanded its services to cover all provinces and districts in the country. However, to further strengthen the health insurance scheme, the following recommendations should be considered.

(i) **Expand population coverage and improve risk pooling of the health insurance scheme.** The HIB could explore opportunities to increase its coverage from the current level of 23% to cover more citizens of Nepal. It could extend coverage to all ultra-poor citizens throughout the country, as it has only been able to cover people in 26 districts. Similarly, the HIB could focus on expanding coverage to the underserved provinces such as Madhesh, Karnali, and Sudurpaschim. To achieve this, the HIB could develop strategies to expand its reach to the underserved areas and work toward increasing enrollment rates. To improve risk pooling of health insurance schemes, HIB could focus on formulating demand generation activities among healthier and formal sector populations.

(ii) **Evaluate financial sustainability and ensure adequate NHIP financing.** The HIB could explore avenues to evaluate the financial sustainability and effectiveness of health insurance schemes. A financial sustainability road map may be required to ensure its long-term viability. Moreover, innovative financing mechanisms could be assessed to increase the fiscal space of the program.

(iii) **Empanelment of health facilities.** The HIB could conduct a feasibility and readiness assessment of health facilities for their empanelment in the health insurance scheme in local-levels without the listed facilities. It could work toward ensuring that all local level governments have at least one health insurance scheme listed health facility to ensure access to NHIP for all.

(iv) **Incorporate updated technology.** The HIB should incorporate updated information and communication technology for the successful implementation of NHIP. Digitalizing the health insurance scheme activities could deliver greater efficiency, effectiveness, and transparency, and allow HIB to serve its beneficiaries better.

(v) **Strengthen HIB.** The HIB could be strengthened, including establishment of a permanent structure, adequate staffing, and automation of claims management. The backlog of claims could threaten the sustainability of the program and result in dwindling confidence of the empaneled health facilities. Moreover, HIB could expand its organization to reflect the federal system of governance in Nepal. Human resources engaged in enrollment of the health insurance scheme members such as enrollment assistants and enrollment officers need to be adequately trained to increase their capacity.

(vi) **Increased ownership by all tiers of government.** Federal, provincial, and local levels must prioritize health insurance scheme in their policies and programs. Attention is required in terms of allocating resources and prioritizing the scheme to cover population in each government's jurisdiction.

(vii) **Explore areas of complementarity with other social protection programs and their information systems.** Opportunities for interoperability and complementarity could be explored with other social protection programs and their information systems such as civil registration and vital statistics, health insurance schemes under the Social Security Fund, and privately managed health insurance programs and systems.

Additionally, explore the feasibility of integration of the health insurance scheme with other vertical programs of similar nature such as medical benefits' program to the impoverished populations.

(viii) **Timely claims settlement.** In response to the growing challenges within the HIB, a series of robust recommendations are proposed to advance the operational framework and service quality. To combat inefficiencies and reduce the margin of error, the adoption of artificial intelligence and machine learning technologies is paramount for automating claims reviews and enhancing fraud detection. Recognizing the critical role of human oversight, the HIB is advised to expand its workforce to manage the increased volume and complexity of claim assessments. Furthermore, the integration of a state-of-the-art, interactive software system promises to revolutionize claims management, enabling a more responsive and client-centric approach. Streamlining claims processing through standardized procedures will ensure uniformity and expedite claim handling. Transitioning to electronic prescriptions will not only streamline the workflow but diminish the likelihood of documentation errors. The efficiency of these measures hinges on the proficiency of the staff, which necessitates comprehensive training in all new systems and processes. To remain competitive and attuned to beneficiaries' needs, the HIB must periodically reassess its benefit offerings, tailoring them to the dynamic health care environment. Finally, to optimize the claims journey, clear ownership must be established, designating specific responsibilities to respective HIB team members at each juncture, thus facilitating accountability and improving overall service delivery.

(ix) **Update benefit package.** The HIB could update its benefit package to ensure fiscal sustainability of the program. Attention is required to work toward developing a comprehensive and relevant package that meets the needs of the population at the same time making the program financially viable. Potential strategies which could be used to update the benefit package are as follows:

(a) *Regular assessment of health care landscapes*: To address the evolving health care landscape, regular assessments are imperative. Identifying emerging medical technologies, treatment approaches, and health care trends is crucial for ensuring the continued relevance and coverage of the benefit package. Establishing a permanent benefit package team at HIB can facilitate ongoing monitoring of health care landscapes.

(b) *Stakeholder engagement*: Collaboration with health care providers, medical experts, patient advocacy groups, and other stakeholders is essential. This collaboration ensures a well-rounded perspective during benefit package revision, helping to fill gaps and improve coverage based on real-world insights.

(c)   **E*vidence-driven decision-making***: Comprehensive data analytics should be employed to analyze claims data, utilization patterns, and cost trends. This data-driven approach can identify areas of high utilization, potential cost-saving opportunities, and gaps in coverage. It can also facilitate the exploration of alternative payment methods, such as Diagnosis-Related Groups, Capitation, or Pay-for-Performance.

(d)   ***Tiered benefit structure***: Implementing a tiered benefit structure that offers different levels of coverage to different service providers can help manage costs while ensuring access to essential treatments. This approach allows for tailored benefits based on the capabilities and specialization of health care facilities.

(e)   ***Cost–benefit analysis***: Before incorporating new treatments or services into the benefit package, thorough cost–benefit analyses should be conducted. These analyses should evaluate potential long-term cost savings against the initial investment required. This ensures that the package remains financially sustainable.

(f)   ***Feedback loop***: Establishing a mechanism for receiving feedback from insurers, service providers, experts, and other stakeholders is essential. This feedback loop should be utilized to drive continuous update and improvement of the benefit package, making it responsive to evolving health care needs and challenges.

APPENDIX 1
DATA SOURCES

This study is a synthesis of both desk review and stakeholders' perspectives. The study was developed in close engagement with officials from the Ministry of Health and Population (MOHP), Ministry of Finance (MOF), and Health Insurance Board (HIB). The study also benefited from in-depth interview findings conducted among the health insurance scheme service users, enrollment assistants, enrollment officers, and provincial coordinators to understand the provincial differences in health insurance scheme's coverage in Koshi, Madhesh, and Gandaki provinces.

This exercise utilized a combination of both quantitative and qualitative methods. A desk review was conducted to analyze the policy environment and stocktaking of relevant studies. Budget data from the Red Book and health insurance scheme data from the HIB were further analyzed. Meanwhile, stakeholders' perspectives were captured through key informant interviews. A draft key informant interview guide was prepared and approval from the MOHP was obtained. Meetings and workshops were conducted to seek the opinion of policymakers and managers working at the MOHP and HIB. Furthermore, an in-depth interview guide was used to implement interviews in Koshi, Madhesh, and Gandaki to explore the factors determining the differences in health insurance scheme coverage.

The stakeholder institutions involved in the interviews and consultations include the MOF (Foreign Aid Division); MOHP–Policy, Planning and Monitoring Division; Health Insurance Board; Provincial Health Directorate–Karnali province; Simta rural municipality; Karnali Province; and Nepal Health Sector Strategy–Foreign, Commonwealth, and Development Office.

APPENDIX 2
TASKS AND APPROACHES

Tasks	Approaches
Introduction: historical development, key achievements, challenges, current status, financing, and governance	Analysis of Red book and data from Health Insurance Board, desk review
Policy environment: chronological analysis of relevant health policies and frameworks	Desk review
Stakeholder's perspectives: overview of key stakeholders such as public providers and policymakers at national and subnational level, professional councils and/or associations, external development partners and the private sector	Seven key informant interviews in each area
Stocktaking of completed and ongoing studies: overview of the relevant completed, ongoing, planned interventions, and studies.	Desk review
Provincial differences in health insurance scheme coverage: key stakeholders including the health insurance scheme service users, enrollment assistants, enrollment officers, district coordinators, and provincial coordinators were interviewed to understand the health insurance scheme coverage in Koshi, Madhesh, and Gandaki	Key informant interviews using interview guide

KEY INFORMANT INTERVIEW 1

Objective

The objective of this key informant interview was to understand the current status, key challenges, and ways forward to improve the universal health coverage/health insurance and its financing mechanism in Nepal.

Time Required: 60 minutes

Guiding Questions

1. Could you please share your experience and knowledge on the historical development of Universal Health Coverage/Health Insurance in Nepal?
2. In your own experience and understanding what are Nepal's key achievements in Universal Health Coverage/Health Insurance?
3. Could you please share the major constraints and challenges being faced while delivering Universal Health Coverage/Health Insurance program in Nepal?
4. How the Universal Health Coverage/Health Insurance program is being implemented in Nepal (governance)?
5. What is the current status and priority of GoN in Universal Health Coverage/Health Insurance in Nepal?
6. Is the current policy environment sufficient to improve the coverage and quality of health care?
7. Are the policies coherent across all spheres of government? If not where are the problems?
8. What additional policy interventions are required to implement the Government of Nepal's commitments?
9. What would be the role of development partners to strengthen the implementation of Universal Health Coverage/Health Insurance in Nepal?
10. What would be the role of private sector to strengthen the implementation of Universal?
11. Health Coverage/Health Insurance in Nepal?
12. What would be the role of professional councils to strengthen the implementation of Universal Health Coverage/Health Insurance in Nepal?
13. In your knowledge are there any specific studies conducted or being conducted on Universal Health Coverage/Health Insurance in Nepal?
14. Are the current financial allocations and modalities sufficient? If not, what would be your suggestions to government of Nepal?
15. Any further update and suggestion.

APPENDIX 4
KEY INFORMANT INTERVIEW 2

Objective

The objective of this key informant interview was to understand the factors underlining differences in insured members' coverage in Koshi, Madhesh, and Gandaki.

Time Required: 30–45 minutes

Guiding Questions

1. Could you please share your experience and knowledge on the historical development of health insurance in Nepal?
2. In your own experience and understanding what are Nepal's key achievements in health insurance?
3. Could you please share the major constraints and challenges being faced while delivering health insurance program in Nepal?
4. How the health insurance program is being implemented in Nepal (governance)?
5. What is the current status and priority of GoN in Health Insurance in Nepal?
6. Is the current policy environment sufficient to improve the coverage and quality of health care?
7. Are the policies coherent across all spheres of government? If not, where are the problems?
8. What additional policy interventions are required to implement the GoN's commitments on health insurance?
9. Are the current financial allocations and modalities sufficient? If not, what would be your suggestions to government of Nepal?
10. How is this Province implementing the health insurance scheme (coverage, renewal, providers)?
11. What is your opinion about the health insurance scheme in Nepal? Is it working well? If yes, why? If not, why not?
12. What challenges do you face while enrolling families in the health insurance scheme?
13. What suggestions do you have to address these challenges?
14. Any further updates and suggestions to strengthen health insurance scheme?
15. How long have you been enrolled in the health insurance scheme? If you have renewed, what motivated you to renew your membership?
16. How is your healthcare seeking experience has been since you got enrolled in the health insurance scheme (probe: benefits, drawbacks, challenges, general care experience)?

17. In your opinion, what are the things the HIB should do to strengthen health insurance scheme?
18. In your opinion, what are the challenges insured members face while seeking care as health insurance scheme members?
19. Any additional suggestions?

APPENDIX 5
STUDIES RELATED TO HEALTH INSURANCE IN NEPAL

Name and Date of the Study	Type of Study	Methods Used	Sampling Frame/ Sample Size	Major Findings
Nepal Health Insurance Impact Evaluation: Baseline Basic Report 2014	Impact evaluation based on randomization.	It includes impact evaluation relating to effectiveness of health insurance in improving health outcomes; process evaluation of program's administrative, operational, and financial aspects; and estimate of its cost-effectiveness.	7,521 households from 6 districts. 40 households from 153 rural municipalities in 3 pilot districts (Baglung, Illam, and Kailali) and 14 households from 100 rural municipalities in 3 districts where health insurance was not implemented yet.	Almost 84% of total sample population sought health care services at a health facility (including private and public facilities) Household OOPE for outpatient services, laboratory services, and x-ray services were relatively low. Transportation to and from health facilities was the biggest expense related to outpatient services. A household with a member needing in-patient treatment will spend over 40% of 1 month's income on those services
Assessment of Social Health Insurance Scheme in Selected Districts of Nepal 2018	Mixed-method study	Desk review, secondary analysis, KII, and exit client interviews.	The study area was Kailali, Baglung, and Illam districts. A total of 338 exit client interviews and 54 KIIs were conducted. Purposive sampling was done for KIIs and consecutive sampling was done for exit client interview.	Respondents expressed challenges related to unavailability of drugs, inadequate laboratory services, and inadequate human resources at health facilities. Service providers mentioned that people with health insurance schemes seek health care services at an earlier stage of the disease as compared to those without health insurance scheme

continued on next page

Table *continued*

Name and Date of the Study	Type of Study	Methods Used	Sampling Frame/ Sample Size	Major Findings
Brief Annual Report of HIB FY2018/2019	Observational study	Desk reviews and secondary analysis		This annual report highlighted the following key challenges related to the health insurance scheme: HIB is still running in temporary organizational structure and through staff seconded from MOHP with a few staff under temporary agreement. Health insurance programs like health insurance scheme are fragmented. For example, the government's free health care program is being implemented alongside health insurance scheme. HIB is not able to enroll extremely poor people under health insurance scheme due to lack of identification cards indicating their poverty status (which is the responsibility of Ministry of Cooperatives, Land Management and Poverty Alleviation). Lack of awareness campaigns.
Factors associated with enrollment of households in Nepal's national health insurance program 2019	Cross-sectional survey	Face-to-face interviews with households enrolled in the health insurance scheme and households which are not enrolled in NHIP	Two rural municipalities of Illam district. Sample size: 570 households (275 each)	Enrollment of household was associated with socioeconomic status and presence of chronic illness in the family.

continued on next page

Table *continued*

Name and Date of the Study	Type of Study	Methods Used	Sampling Frame/ Sample Size	Major Findings
Satisfaction survey of insured and policy research on National Health Insurance Program 2020	Cross-sectional study based on purposive sampling	Quantitative and qualitative	Jhapa, Palpa, and Kailali districts. Sample size: 1,227 respondents	There was a statistically significant association among wealth status and enrollment in health insurance scheme and presence of chronic health condition in a family and enrollment in NHIP. Respondents from richest economic category were less likely to get enrolled in health insurance scheme as compared to those in poorest economic category. Challenges include inadequate human resources in empaneled health facilities, difficulty in seeking referral services, identification of people under extreme poverty, enrollment assistants not satisfied with their incentives, high dropout rate, untimely reimbursements of claims made, inadequate stock of essential medicines, and shortage of medical doctors. Informants suggested that awareness regarding benefits of health insurance scheme should be increased, and health facilities should have adequate health infrastructure.

continued on next page

Table *continued*

Name and Date of the Study	Type of Study	Methods Used	Sampling Frame/ Sample Size	Major Findings
Survey Report on Governance Reform of Health Insurance Board 2020	Observational study based on qualitative design	Desk reviews and consultations with key stakeholders		This study pointed out the following challenges relating to governance of HIB: Lack of adequate staffing at local level. Not all medicines listed in national health insurance scheme are available in pharmacies of empaneled hospitals, compelling insured ones to purchase these from other facilities. Claim process is complex and time- consuming. Lack of financial autonomy from HIB. Separate health insurance packages not integrated with health insurance scheme are being implemented by ministries and their departments. Lack of motivation and capacity-building activities for staff. Lack of clarity in organizational structure of the HIB.

continued on next page

Table *continued*

Name and Date of the Study	Type of Study	Methods Used	Sampling Frame/ Sample Size	Major Findings
Status and determinants of enrollment and dropout of health insurance in Nepal: an explorative study 2020	Mixed-method study	Quantitative aspect included secondary analysis of data related to enrollment and dropout. Qualitative aspect included focus group discussions.	Enrollment assistants in Bardiya, Chitwan, and Gorkha districts were purposively selected	Enrollment assistants were not able to properly educate people about the importance of SHI while clarifying the difference between general insurance and health insurance. There was no proper coordination between branches of HIB at the provincial and local levels. The reasons for not enrolling in the health insurance scheme and which also result in dropout are insufficiency of medicines and other essential medical supplies, people have to wait for a long period of time to seek health care, poorly maintained infrastructure, discouragement because of the unprofessional behavior of health service provider.
Awareness on Social Health Insurance Scheme among Locals in Bhaktapur Municipality 2020	Cross-sectional study	Face-to-face interviews	A sample size of 385 respondents was randomly selected from 5 different wards of Bhaktapur municipality.	Majority of respondents were aware about SHI. Enrollment assistants and female community health volunteers were main source of information. Approximately 91.9% of total respondents wanted to renew their health insurance scheme in the future.

HIB = Health Insurance Board, KII = key informant interview, NHIP = National Health Insurance Program, SHI = social health insurance, OOPE= out-of-pocket expenditures.
Source: Findings from authors' desk review.

REFERENCES

The Asia Foundation. 2017. A survey of the Nepali people in 2017. San Francisco: The Asia Foundation.

_____ . 2018. A Survey of the Nepali People in 2018. San Francisco: The Asia Foundation.

_____ . 2020. A Survey of the Nepali People in 2020. San Francisco: The Asia Foundation.

_____ . 2022. A Survey of the Nepali People in 2022. San Francisco: The Asia Foundation.

Asian Development Bank. 2019. Macroeconomic Update: Nepal. Manila.

_____ . 2023. Macroeconomic Update: Nepal 2023. Manila.

The Constitution of Nepal 2015. Kathmandu.

Ghimire, M., R. Ayer, and M. Kondo. 2018. Cumulative Incidence, Distribution, and Determinants of Catastrophic Health Expenditure in Nepal: Results from Living Standards Survey. *International Journal for Equity in Health*. 17:23.

Ghimire, P., V.P. Sapkota, and K.A. Poudyal. 2019. Factors Associated with Enrollment of Households in Nepal's National Health Insurance Program. *International Journal of Health Policy and Management*. 8 (11). 636–645.

Giri, D., U. Pyakurel, and C.L. Pandey. 2020. A Survey of the Nepali People in 2020. Hattiban (Lalitpur): Kathmandu University.

Government of Nepal. 2017. National Health Policy. Kathmandu.

Government of Nepal, Central Bureau of Statistics, and UNICEF Nepal. 2020. Nepal Multiple Indicator Cluster Survey 2019 Survey Findings Report. Kathmandu.

Government of Nepal, Department of Health Services. Health Management Information System: Population Projection, 2014/2015–2019/2020. Kathmandu.

Government of Nepal, Health Insurance Board. 2018. Annual Report for FY2017/2018. Kathmandu.

_____ . 2019. Brief Annual Report for FY2018/2019. Kathmandu.

_____ . 2021. A Presentation on National Health Insurance Program. Kathmandu.

_____ . 2022. A Presentation on National Health Insurance Program at the Joint Annual Review of the Ministry of Health and Population. Kathmandu.

_____ . 2022. Annual Report of Health Insurance Program for FY2021/2022. Kathmandu.

_____ . 2023. Presentation on Benefit Package Revision: Current Approach and Challenges. Kathmandu.

_____ . 2023. Presentation on Current Approach to Provider Management and Provider Contract. Kathmandu.

_____ . 2023. Presentation on Operational Status, Issues, Challenges, and Ways Forward. Kathmandu.

_____ . 2023. Presentation on Progress and Update on National Health Insurance Program. Kathmandu.

Government of Nepal, Ministry of Finance. Red Book for Respective Fiscal Years.

_____ . 2015. Red Book for Fiscal Year 2014/2015. Kathmandu.

_____ . 2020. Health Sector Budget for Fiscal Year 2019/2020. Kathmandu.

_____ . 2022. Economic Survey 2021/2022. Kathmandu.

Government of Nepal, Ministry of Health and Population. 1997. Second Long-Term Health Plan, 1997–2017. Kathmandu.

_____ . 2022. Nepal National Health Accounts 2017/2018. Kathmandu.

_____ . 2023. Draft of Strategic Road Map of Health Insurance Program 2024– 2030. Kathmandu.

Government of Nepal, Ministry of Health and Population; New ERA; and ICF. 2017. Nepal Demographic and Health Survey 2016. Kathmandu.

_____ . Nepal Demographic and Health Survey 2022. Kathmandu.

Government of Nepal, National Statistics Office. 2023. National Population and Housing Census 2021 National Report. Kathmandu.

Health Insurance Act 2017. Kathmandu.

International Monetary Fund (IMF). 2023. Nepal IMF Country Report NO. 23/158. Washington, DC.

Lohani, G.R., G.N. Sharma, H. Bhatt, T. Suresh, and D.R. Ghimire. 2020. Budget Analysis of Health Sector (2020), Ministry of Health and Population and Nepal Health Sector Support Program. Kathmandu.

Mcintyre D., F. Meheus, and J.A. Rottingen. 2017. What level of domestic government health expenditure should we aspire to for universal health coverage? *Health Economics, Policy and Law.* 12 (2). 125–137.

National Planning Commission. 2016. Nepal and the Millennium Development Goals Final Status Report 2000-2015. Kathmandu.

_____. 2020. Nepal: Sustainable Development Goals Progress Assessment Report 2016-2019. Kathmandu.

Nepal Health Research Council. 2018. Assessment of social health insurance scheme in selected districts of Nepal. Kathmandu.

Public Health and Research Development Center Nepal and Korea International Cooperation Agency. 2020. Insuree Satisfaction Survey and Policy Research in National Health Insurance Program. Kathmandu.

Ranabhat, C.L., R. Subedi, and S. Karn. 2020. Status and determinants of enrollment and dropout of health insurance in Nepal: an explorative study. *Cost Effectiveness and Resource Allocation.* 18 (40).

Shrestha, M.V., N. Manandhar, M. Dhimal, and S.K. Joshi. 2020. Awareness on Social Health Insurance Scheme among Locals in Bhaktapur Municipality. *Journal of Nepal Health Research Council.* 18 (3).

Stoermer, M. et al. 2012. Review of Community-based Health Insurance Initiatives in Nepal. Kathmandu: GIZ Health Sector Support Program.

Wang, X. and Z. Cheng. 2020. Cross-Sectional Studies: Strengths, Weakness, and Recommendations. *An Overview of Study Design and Statistical Considerations.* 158 (1). S65–S71.

World Bank. 2007. Social Health Insurance for Developing Nations. Washington, DC.

_____. 2014. Nepal Health Insurance Impact Evaluation: Baseline Basic Report. Kathmandu.

_____. 2020. Nepal-Joint World Bank-International Monetary Fund Debt Sustainability Analysis (English). Washington, DC.

_____. 2023. World Development Indicators. Washington, DC.

World Health Organization. 2023. Global Health Expenditure Database. Geneva.

World Health Organization and the World Bank. 2019. Global Monitoring Report on Financial Protection in Health 2019. Geneva.

www.ingramcontent.com/pod-product-compliance
Lightning Source LLC
Chambersburg PA
CBHW042034220326
41599CB00045BA/7388